The Faith Abroad

Faith and the Future
General Editor: David Nicholls

Choices
Ethics and the Christian
David Brown

The Church and the Nation
The Case for Disestablishment
Peter Cornwell

Pastoral Care and the Parish
Peter Davie

The Faith Abroad
John D. Davies

Church, Ministry and Unity
A Divine Commission
James E. Griffiss

The Authority of Divine Love
Richard Harries

The Bible
Fountain and Well of Truth
John Muddiman

Faith, Prayer and Devotion
Ralph Townsend

Sacraments and Liturgy
The Outward Signs
Louis Weil

The Faith Abroad

John D. Davies

Basil Blackwell · Oxford

© John D. Davies 1983

First published 1983
Basil Blackwell Publisher Limited
108 Cowley Road, Oxford OX4 1JF, England

British Library Cataloguing in Publication Data

Davies, John D.
   The faith abroad.
   1. Missions
   I. Title
   266   BV2061

   ISBN 0-631-13183-3
   ISBN 0-631-13221-X Pbk

Typeset by Cambrian Typesetters,
Farnborough, Hants
Printed in Great Britain by
T. J. Press Ltd, Padstow

Contents

People in Mission

Foreword

This book is one of a series whose writers consider some important aspects of Christianity in the contemporary scene, and in so doing they draw inspiration from the Catholic revival in the Anglican Communion which began in Oxford one hundred and fifty years ago. This revival — with its thinkers, pastors, prophets, social reformers and not a few who have been held to be saints — has experienced changes in the understanding of the Christian faith since the time of the Tractarians and has none the less borne witness to themes which are deep and unchanging. Among these are the call to holiness, the communion of saints, the priesthood of the church and its ministers, and a sacramental religion, both other worldly and with revolutionary claims upon man's social life.

I am myself convinced that the renewal of the church for today and tomorrow needs a deep recovery of these themes of Catholic tradition and a vision of their contemporary application. The books of this series are designed towards this end, and I am sure that readers will be grateful for the help they give. Many are thirsty but 'the well is deep'.

Michael Ramsey   +

He does what is done in many places
what he does other
    he does after the mode
of what has always been done.
What did he do other
      recumbent at the garnished supper?
What did he do yet other
      riding the Axile Tree?

The conclusion of *The Anathemata* by David Jones[1]

Preface

This book is about the effect of the Oxford Movement, and about overseas missions. At first sight, these two themes seem to be like old outposts of Empire, belonging securely in the vanished world of the nineteenth century. I have neither the knowledge nor the opportunity to survey the mission work of Anglican Catholics as a detailed historical study; but I am convinced that there are great truths and values in this inheritance which are highly relevant to us as we seek to find the appropriate mission action for these days in Britain as well as overseas.

I have to be very selective. I can testify only to a few of the truths that have made some sense to me, both as an overseas missionary in Southern Africa and as a trainer of missionaries at Selly Oak in Birmingham. In both these roles, I have been glad to be closely involved with the United Society for the Propagation of the Gospel, the oldest Anglican missionary society, and the society which is most used as a channel for missionary energy by people who see themselves as inheritors of the Oxford Movement tradition. But the USPG is not simply an Agency of Anglo-Catholicism, and I expect that some British Anglo-Catholics will find that issues which at present cause them most excitement do not get much attention in this book.

I have used the phrase 'overseas mission'; but there are many areas overseas from Britain, especially in North America and Australasia, which are no longer the direct concern of British Anglican missionary societies. Our area of concern is the so-called 'Third World'; this also is an unsatisfactory term, but I cannot think of a better one. The 'Third World' is, in any case, a vast and varied area;

and I have limited myself very largely to examples from Central and Southern Africa to illustrate my themes, rather than try to select evenly from all over the planet.

I am specially indebted to the writings of three bishops. John Taylor, for me, opened up a whole new way of relating Christian faith and traditional human wisdom, especially in *The Primal Vision* and *The Go-Between God*.[2] Lesslie Newbigin's missionary theology permeated the whole environment at the Selly Oak Colleges for several years; he managed to summarize much of this in his valuable book *The Open Secret*.[3] We who breathed the same air with him at Selly Oak can never know when we are quoting him, and he has certainly found his way onto these pages. E. R. Morgan, who was the first warden of the College of the Ascension at Selly Oak, was of a generation which is easily overlooked in these days. The sheer wisdom and continuing relevance of the books which he was writing and editing fifty years ago are good evidence of the solid value of the tradition which we are commemorating in this series.

My wife, Shirley, has made this book physically and spiritually possible — both by getting the typing done within a tight deadline and by continually insisting that a book about mission has to reflect God's bias towards people who have had little benefit from the conventional systems of society.

To be on the staff of the Selly Oak Colleges is an extraordinary experience. Every day brings some new story or insight from the world church, and the teachers receive more than they give. This book, to a large extent, reflects what I have been trying to communicate there over several years; but much of it is what has been communicated to me, by students and other colleagues. I cannot possibly acknowledge each debt. I am deeply grateful for what I have received, especially from people of traditions other than my own. I think that this is not incompatible with the way in which I find that I have been sent back to affirm some of the values of the tradition which I myself would claim to belong to.

Anglo-Catholicism has appeared to be a tightly defined and articulated system, where you know where you stand and where your principles are clear. As I have tried to write this book, I have come to realize, with delight and frustration, just how unpredictable, contradictory and unclassifiable this tradition actually is. Any account of it that is systematic and coherent will misrepresent it. There is a kind of Anglo-Catholicism which I, who claim to be part of this movement, feel to be limiting and unattractive. There is a kind, also, which to me is truly Christlike, which is secure at its centre and therefore is splendidly reckless about categories, qualifications, systems, and deservings. Tommy Morris was a greatly loved priest in this tradition, of the Church in Wales, and I take his summary of the matter as a kind of motto for this book: 'God pours his grace through very leaky buckets.' If Anglo-Catholicism has done any good, it will be because of what it has dripped out rather than what it has held in. I hope that, in this respect, this book may not be untypical of its subject!

John D. Davies
Llanelwy/St Asaph and Froncysyllte
.

INTRODUCTION

1 Themes of Mission

The Catholic movement within Anglicanism has always been a system of values: therefore it has always been a missionary movement. As a self-conscious movement, it is reckoned to take its start from John Keble's Assize Sermon in Oxford, on 14 July 1833. Whatever one's view of the content of that preaching, there can be no doubt that the sermon, and the tracts that followed, had a basically missionary character. The authors were communicating in public, addressing themselves to society at large; they were concerned to bring about change, to persuade, to influence, to clarify truth and to expose untruth. They had a mission. Further, their mission was not merely a religious campaign; although for much of the time the movement seems to have been limited to religious issues, originally and fundamentally it sprang from a concern for the right ordering of the whole of society.

Such a missionary movement could not operate for long without developing institutions; it developed its network of loyalties through the existing structures of the church, and it gave birth to new institutions for propagating its ideals and for the formation of its agents. It aimed at change, and it measured its success by the numbers and categories of persons whom it managed to incorporate into its programme of change.

We have to acknowledge that the Oxford Movement does not at first sight appear to have been particularly concerned with some of the things that most interest missionaries. In assembling his selection of characteristic Tractarian writings, *The Mind of the Oxford Movement*, Dr Owen Chadwick chose to include only one paragraph on the theme of 'Evangelism'; and this, by Isaac Williams, stresses that the gospel is commended not by words but by the Church's obedience.[4] The Tractarians' belief in 'reserve in communicating religious knowledge' meant that they were thoroughly suspicious of some programmes and methods of evangelism. They strove for the renewal of the Church of England in faith and obedience; they were concerned for the integrity of the church, in its intellectual life and in its spiritual and intuitive life — they claimed the skills of poets as well as those of intellectual debaters. They were concerned primarily with issues which, in the first instance, were of interest within the formal organization of the church and made most sense to members of the clerical profession. These would not normally be called 'missionary' interests. None the less, these interests and issues led to a movement which had a profound effect on mission. Without any special pleading, we can claim that the Catholic movement within Anglicanism has made its mark primarily as a missionary movement.

By its very nature, a missionary movement is always ill-at-ease with its boundaries. It attracts and encourages people who do not want to be limited to what is known and familiar and permitted. It provides itself with marching orders which will justify its desire to extend its influence, which will legitimize its refusal to yield to the defences of people who say, 'This is none of your business', and which will give holy sanction to its refusal to accept convenient and customary categories behind which institutions pursue their immediate interests without disturbance. So the Catholic movement found itself challenging and crossing boundaries, both of social order and of geographical demarcation. It became a movement concerned with social responsibility, and it shared powerfully in the total European venture of international church extension.

In the last 150 years, mission has been a feature of a very wide range of sectors and emphases within the British and European framework. It is almost too easy to propose that, in Christian mission in this era, the churches have merely been climbing in on a fashion of aggressive

2

self-confidence, a racial ambitiousness which has frantically been searching for geographical and technological frontiers to cross. This would be an attractive explanation, if it were not for the habit of penitence and corporate self-criticism which the church has never been quite able to shake off. It is, however, certainly true to say that the Western churches have been part of a general Western programme of expansion, and in this sense the Church has not been the only missionary movement. And it is also true to say that within Christendom, the Catholic movement has not had a monopoly of missionary enterprise. It is not part of our present intention to suggest that the Catholic movement has been specially committed or virtuous or successful in comparison with other formations within the total Christian spectrum. But we are suggesting that there are certain particular features which are worth noting, both in the ideological equipment and in the historical experience of Anglican Catholicism; and these may be of interest within a much wider range of Christian enterprise.

2   A God who Changes Things

There are two primary themes which are of particular importance within Catholic consciousness and which should be expected to make a difference within a Catholic style of mission. These themes are common to the whole Christian movement, of course, because they are fundamental within New Testament proclamation. All Christians would accept that they are elements within our total equipment of faith: but for people within the Catholic tradition they are almost a natural instinct, a basic mindset into which other elements fit. So, in principle, they should shape and guide a Catholic sense of mission, and they should predispose members of this tradition to take mission seriously. In the main body of this book, we shall find that these two themes continually make their appearance and contribute to our judgements concerning the church's practice of mission. In this chapter and the next, I intend merely to introduce them without developing their implications in detail.

The first of these Catholic instincts is the instinct for a God who changes things. This is at the heart of the Eucharist: it is what Catholicism has most characteristically stood for. Now, it is possible to try to domesticate this God who changes things, to restrict his ability to change things, to limit it to just the one point where change is covenanted, to exhaust its meaning by tying it to the one sacramental act where the power-bearers of the church feel that they have the process under control. This separates the sacrament from the rest of life, so that God has an area within which he can safely make changes and outside which his role is to keep things as they are. This approach is well summed up in the remark: 'We're all in favour of change, provided that it doesn't make any difference.'[5]

This is one of many points at which the Catholic movement has offered a divided witness. This is not a difference between doctrinal parties but a matter of emphasis in the application of basic doctrines. All Catholics would agree that the Mass is the point where God's power to change has its covenanted place in the world. But is the Mass a way of seeing God's activity in the world as a whole, or is it miraculously different from anything which takes place in the rest of the world? Can the whole natural order be seen as potentially sacramental, or are the sacraments interruptions of the natural order?

It would be foolish to deny that the latter emphasis has been strong within the Catholic movement; but I suggest that it should not be seen as essential to it. In fact, its effect is exactly the same as the disastrous tendency within Calvinism to separate the order of grace from the order of nature; it is this which gives religious sanction to the unwillingness of most of the Dutch Reformed Churches in South Africa to make any criticism of the disorders of the state. It may, perhaps, have a certain logical place within Calvinism, but is inconsistent with the whole ethos of Catholicism. It means that instead of seeing God's activity in Christ as a claiming of the whole world, we limit God's activity to a substitutional arrangement; he works for change in the bread *instead of* bringing about change in the universe as a whole. But this is not the way of incarnation. We believe that God took flesh in one human being in order to show what is possible for all human beings; he does what he does with bread to show what is possible for all creation. The small, singular place of God's presence and action is a microcosm of the whole. So the Eucharist is the continual reminder of God's purpose to change, not only to change bread into body (how exactly, we don't know), but sinners into saints (how exactly, we don't know), and the kingdoms of this world into the kingdom of our God and of his Christ (how exactly, we don't know).

In this insisting on God's purpose to change, the Catholic

movement is in accord with one of the main features of the witness of Jesus. In episode after episode in the gospels, we see the effect of Jesus' presence as transformation. In his healings, his exorcisms, his controversies and his teachings, he was not just strengthening an existing state of goodness, nor was he restoring people to a previous equilibrium. Healing at the hands of Jesus was not just treatment, it was salvation. It was a new thing breaking into the existing arrangements. It brought change. And therefore it was received with most enthusiasm by those who were getting least advantage out of the existing arrangements. Jesus was good news for the poor, the outsider, the demon-possessed, the insecure and messed-up people who were victims of society's conventions and boundaries. He brought change.

When, for instance, Jesus started looking for people who could bear witness to the difference he made, he did not select people who already had influence; to do so would have meant merely putting a new movement on the market alongside all the others, using existing channels and methods. He went to an area on the fringe of the national territory — Galilee — and got hold of people who had no particular social significance — fishermen. To them, he gave the invitation: come with me, and I will make you fishers of men — you will become people of influence and significance. To bring about such change was inevitably controversial; the gospels record the sharpening pattern of conflict between those who resisted change and the one who brought change. And those who needed change tended often to get caught in the middle.

The apostolic church continued to be a change-bringer. It did not merely copy Jesus' activity. It translated Jesus' activity into new situations. For Jesus, the problem could be summarized as: Is it right to treat 'sinners' (including lepers, haemorrhaging women, pagans, and stooges of the occupying power) with the same personal care and priority that are given to scribes and synagogue officials? For the apostolic church, the same basic problem came out in the shape of: Is it right to accept barbarian gentile pagans into

6

the fellowship on the same terms as cultured law-centred Jews? In each case, the powerfully transforming answer was — Yes. This, more than its worship, its ethic, or even its doctrine, was the fundamentally new feature of the apostolic church. It formed an unprecedented and unique social mix. This was the main way in which Christ was seen as a transforming power. It is no accident that Paul's most profound account of love occurs in the course of a document which bears witness to the scarcely imaginable variety of human types that found themselves called to rub shoulders with each other in the church in Corinth (I Corinthians 13).

If the power of change is truly the power of God, it will be a change which changes us ourselves. We will be required not only to be agents and proclaimers of change; we will be on the receiving end of it also. This is a test question for Anglican Catholicism. It can so honour and isolate the one special moment of change which it recognizes, that it becomes a barrier to all other change. It can encourage its devotees to be extremely careful of the company they keep and the places where they go; they search for a church which suits them, which fits them as they are, which demands the least possible change from them. The sectarian church, of whatever label, is co-opted into a conspiracy against conversion, especially that kind of conversion which is represented by the meeting with a person of a different language and style.

One of the most important discoveries of the New Testament church was that the practice of mission changes not only the world outside and people outside the church: mission changes the church itself. The Church is continually being modified, re-shaped, and enlarged by the new persons who come within its range. It does not merely go out to attract new people into a ready-prepared set of conventions and traditions. That would be proselytism, not mission; such a programme sees other people as a commodity to be consumed. The missionary church goes out to others in the power of the Spirit who, according to the promise of the Gospel, leads us into all truth (John 16:13): it goes out so that it can itself learn about the God who is at work in the world seeking to be known, enabling the transformation that will fulfil the purposes of creation.

In New Testament times, the Jewish establishment within the Church had to discover, by a hard way, that Christ meant as much change for Jew as for Gentile, and that catholicity could not be based on a programme of assimilating new groups into patterns already formed by the old. Jews found themselves having to adjust to a church which had been profoundly modified by its Gentile mission. Paul wrestled with the implication of this in chapters 9—11 of Romans — a passage crucial for any church-in-mission. The conversion of Cornelius leads to the conversion of Peter (Acts 10).

Always this pattern comes to disturb any church which takes mission seriously — and mission, in this sense, can be as commonplace a thing as an open youth club. The Catholic awareness of God's programme of transformation surely should be one of the church's main resources for coping with and interpreting such change. It can equip people with the kind of adaptability and courage which Robert Kennedy commended at the end of a visit to South Africa shortly before his assassination, when he said to the South African public, 'Change is coming to you, be sure of that; what matters is whether you co-operate with it or resist it, whether you receive it as an enemy or a friend.'

So a church-in-mission will find itself being changed. And, by definition, a church-in-mission is in business to bring about change in persons and in society. But it has to discriminate. Not all change is of God. Sometimes, for example, in its opposition to a monstrous novelty like racism, the church has to be aggressively conservative. But, particularly in its mission in new cultural contexts overseas, the church is likely to be saved from a temptation which has sometimes influenced Anglican Catholicism in Britain, namely the temptation to achieve salvation by recapturing a past golden age. That is one form of change, and it is an attractive option where the church has a long cultural history. In England, the appeal to a long-past medieval

8

blessedness had considerable attraction. But only a minority of people could acquire the particular bundle of aware-nesses which would make this appeal a really living motive; it required a degree of historical informedness which was unattainable for most people, as well as being very distant from their immediate conditions and problems. But, because of the power of this informed minority, a romantic backward-looking motive made a vast and visible difference on English churchmanship. This was far from being all nonsense, but there are at least two dangers here. One is the danger of being very selective in one's use of history; for instance, it is difficult to glorify medieval England without becoming insensitive to the claims of those other communities in Britain for whom England's dominance was not a glory but a disaster. The other danger is the more general and insidious one, that we become part of a general religious conspiracy which seeks to persuade people that deliverance from our present problems will be achieved by a recapturing of the past. This is perhaps an understand-able reaction to the various kinds of utopianism which have been proclaiming a salvation in the future by means of the automatic working out of technological or economic or political processes. But it is incompatible with belief in God as creator, who continues to be creator in the present age; it is incompatible with belief in God as saviour who saves *this* world, the only world which we can really know; it is incompatible with belief in God as the Spirit who leads us into a truth which is ahead of us.

The greatest practical influence which steered Anglican Catholicism from this seductive by-path was the experience of overseas mission; there, it had to discover its place and achieve its relevance in cultural contexts where no appeal to a national past was any use. Overseas mission was, and is, a continual jolt to the system, particularly of a Christian tradition which is conscious of its involvement in national history and culture. The newer churches say to us, 'Don't ignore this past of yours; but don't think that your national past is essential to a Christian identity, because we can show you that it isn't.' Catholicism knows in its bones that it would be fundamentally betraying its foundation in the apostolic church if it ever allowed a system of grades of membership in which superior status could be claimed by those who happen to inherit a longer tradition of Christianity. To be true to its own doctrines, it had to insist that the younger churches have equal honour with the older churches.

The Catholic understanding of change strengthens the positive motive for mission. According to the Eucharistic model, change does not necessarily involve destruction. It is not because there is something wrong with bread that bread is chosen to be changed into Body. Bread is chosen to be Body because of bread's potential, bread's basic goodness. Granted that, in all our present experience, saints are made out of sinners, the process of saint-making does not absolutely depend on a supply of sinners. In fact, most of us find that we have more problems with the conversion of our goodness than of our badness — as is made very clear in Christ's dealing with Pharisees. The process of transformation may be more dramatic where there is obvious and massive evil, leprosy, demon-possession, and so on. But the evidence of the Gospels is that Jesus found as much obstruction to his programme in the obstinate common sense of his disciples as in the raging opposition of the demons.

God's programme of completing creation, of bringing in his kingdom on earth, continues to be a programme of change even if there is not massive evil to combat. Eucharist is not less relevant in the classless society than it is on the edge of undisguised hell. Grace does not have to assume that nature is, by definition, evil. Catholicism, therefore, on the whole neither needs nor seeks evidence of dramatic conflict between the forces of good and evil. It may be in danger of complacency, but it avoids pressurizing people to experience a conflict more extreme than their particular spiritual situation requires. In a full claiming of Christian symbolism, we do not have to limit ourselves to images such as 'redemption' and 'salvation'; important as these images are, they are still fundamentally negative, they concentrate our attention on the evil state of things from which we are delivered.

Any programme of mission has to decide how far it comes as destroyer and how far it comes as fulfiller, how far it comes as critic and how far it comes as consecrator. The deepest disagreements among missionaries, and among mission students, centre on this sort of question. And many of the present tensions within younger churches overseas arise from a sense that an earlier generation of mission agents overplayed the critic-function and persuaded people that their whole native culture was that from which they needed salvation. There are good examples where Protestant missions have avoided this danger, and no doubt Catholic missions have failed to avoid it: but the Catholic emphasis ought, logically, to be a safeguard. It insists that God's purpose is not confined to the negative process of salvation; indeed the real work starts only when that process is over, for the final purpose of God's programme of change is that we human beings are made partakers of the divine nature, and are involved in the corporate life of the Blessed Trinity.

The practical upshot of this is that a Catholic-minded church in mission will recognize realistically all obstacles which obstruct, conceal or deny this final purpose; but it will not have a persistent need to sniff out more and more manifestations of evil so that people can have an un-exhaustible supply of nastiness to be delivered from. It will not need to feel all the time that it has to be in business as a salvation-agency, and therefore it will not need to encourage in its members that instinct which tells us to identify ourselves in terms of those features which make us feel different from or privileged over other persons. Only when it has sorted out its motives at this point can a church avoid being part of the problem of human disunity and start to become part of God's answer.

3 The Truth of the Body

The second major theme which the Catholic movement brings to its mission work is the theme of the Body of Christ.

Again, it is necessary to take this theme with full seriousness and not to satisfy ourselves by using it merely as a kind of token or emblem of our tradition.

Those who claim the image of 'the Body' most enthusiastically often seem to treat it as a kind of privilege, a source of pride, almost a badge of achievement. Of course, to be the Body of Christ is indeed an extraordinary privilege. But first of all the term needs to be seen as a function, an operation, rather than as just a title. A body is, first and foremost, a person's functioning, and its soundness has to be measured in functional terms. A body is truly a body if it communicates, operates, experiences, and registers sense-perceptions efficiently. The Body of Christ is validated as such not primarily by its qualifications but by its operational effectiveness. The Body of Christ is the Body of Christ if it enables the word of Jesus to be heard, the activity of Jesus to be performed, and the experience of Jesus to be suffered. If it doesn't, it may perhaps be a 'mystical body' — whatever that may be, and if the phrase is not a contradiction in terms — but it will not be what a body is primarily supposed to be, namely a functional body.

Now, here is an aspect of the Catholic inheritance which is fundamental to mission, and which the image of the Body should help us to cherish. It is this — the most significant form of truth is embodied truth. To be embodied means to be historical, and to be historical means to be to some extent limited, tied to a time and a place. To be embodied means to be functional, operational, and to some extent subject to verification by observation. A great deal of our education tends to suggest that we are closer to significant truth when we are dealing with generalized truth, such as can apply anywhere without adaptation or modification. This is classical truth; with a living language, you often cannot be totally certain that you have got your expression 'correct', because correctness varies from area to area and is constantly on the move. The correctness of a classical-language sentence structure does not vary according to whether it is being studied in Tokyo or Torquay. The same applies even more to the modern form of classics, namely mathematics.

I am not wanting to devalue these universal forms of truth: they represent something which is valid and essential — although living-language education still bears scars where it has been bent to fit classical-language norms. But we do need to ask, what is the appropriate model for theological truth? Is it timeless, definitive, universal? Is the best model for theological truth to be found in the disciplines of classics and mathematics? And how is theological truth to be verified? At the risk of being easily misconstrued, I want to urge that we take this image of Body seriously, and say that truth is most significantly truth in theology when it enables the proper functioning of the Body. The truth of God is the word-made-flesh.

Many new Anglican service books require the reader of scripture to conclude the reading by saying, 'This is the word of the Lord'. Such a statement is a reversion to the ways of the Old Testament. So is the habit of describing the Bible itself as the Word of God. For disciples of the incarnate Lord, no collection of sounds, or of black marks on white paper, can properly be the Word of God. We misrepresent the revelation in Christ if we give the impression that the Word of God now is anything less than a functional, active, personal presence in the world, continuing to communicate in the world by the whole range of communication used by the incarnate Word in the flesh of Jesus. So where do we look for our models of truth in theology,

13

if theology is to be true to this embodied word? Not, I suggest, to the classics and the pure sciences, but to the technologies. We would say that a theological truth is to be valued insofar as it enables the functioning of the Body of Christ for the purpose for which it is intended, namely the forwarding of the Kingdom of God which Jesus inaugurated, or, in a phrase much cherished within the Catholic movement, the extension of the incarnation.

At Pentecost, the purpose of God starts to be embodied in the disciple-community. Theology develops as a resource for that community in the fulfilling of that purpose. In so far as theology works in that purpose, it is true to its basic mandate. Engineering laboratories and architectural schools rightly and properly generate bright ideas and dream up novel fantasies: but these then have to be tested out by the hard criteria of cost-effectiveness and operational practice. It has now become commonplace to allege that there was a kind of untruth in the notion of high-rise flats as major resource for urban housing. Perhaps it is fair to criticize the Death-of-God theology on roughly similar grounds, namely that it was dysfunctional to the actual operation of the Body of Christ. This is certainly not a plea for mere conservatism; that can be equally dysfunctional. Nor is it a plea for trimming our theological exposition to what people can readily accept (which is, in fact, merely a simple form of conservatism).

A functional theology is a theology which will enable the Body of Christ to be what it is called to be, to do what it is called to do, to say what it is called to say, and to suffer what it is called to suffer, in this particular place and time. It has, therefore, to be a theology which will enable poor, weak, and incompetent human beings to recognize and stand up against the demons, the powers of darkness and the manipulative tyrants which resist the Kingdom of God in our day, and which treat God's children as a commodity to be consumed or a prey to be hunted. It has to be a theology which does not by-pass the demands of intellectual integrity and which does not depend on people remaining compliant and immature; but it has also to be a

14

theology which recognizes that embodied truth operates through emotion, intuition, imagination and will, as well as through intellect. A theology which short-sells people on the intellectual level is a defective theology, but so is a theology which fails to grasp the imagination and the will.

Christian theology must be judged primarily by whether it serves the purpose of him who is its origin, its subject and its centre, namely Jesus Christ. The necessary implication of this is that any theology which is not in principle a missionary theology is to that extent not theology; and any theology which implies that it can be verified merely by being thought and discussed, without needing to be acted and suffered, is also to that extent not theology. The actual content of our theology insists that this must be so, for this pattern is at the heart of our theology's foundation documents; these insist that truth is something that is done, and that the knowledge of God is measured in terms of right relationships of charity and justice between persons and groups (e.g. I John 1:5−2:6).

All this suggests that an operational theology is likely to be conservative; this is true. Just as ordinary domestic architecture tends to be conservative, because ordinary builders building ordinary houses for ordinary people dare not take many risks with untested materials and equipment, so an operational theology knows that, at the level of imagination and intuition, the traditional images run deep and that, if they are removed, people are likely to be less effective as Christian agents. But this conservative tendency must never be allowed to misrepresent that basic purpose, which is not to preserve but to transform.

The purpose of theology is not just to serve the interests of the Church as the Church at present sees them. The purpose of the Church is not just self-maintenance; nor is it simply to ensure its own growth. Neither of these projects necessarily serve Christ's purpose of transformation, though at best they contribute to it. Those who give supreme importance to their sense of membership of the Body of Christ may find themselves under judgement from a truly operational theology which takes the embodying of Christian truth seriously.

The distinction which I am trying to make is well illuminated by a story told by Canon Allchin:

> One day the Abbot [of a Greek monastery] took me to see the monastery library. It was not a very large collection of books. There were a lot of elderly, well-used volumes of the Fathers. 'Here,' said the Abbot, 'is a book which you give to beginners.' 'Here is a work which is useful for someone who is depressed.' 'Here is a book which will give very clear instructions about the Jesus Prayer.' Any Westerner showing you round this collection of books . . . would have said: 'Here is an interesting sixth-century text.' 'This writer shows influences from the Syrian tradition.' 'Here is a work important in the later development of Hesychasm.' We look at books chronologically and classify them in terms of influences and development. To the Abbot they all had a simultaneous existence and composed a simultaneous order . . . He showed me the library rather in the way in which an expert gardener might show you his collection of books on gardening, or a cook a collection of cookery books.[6]

For the 'Westerner' that Canon Allchin conjures up, the books do, of course, serve a useful purpose; they provide the necessary raw material out of which can be made new books, new theses, new employment within the academic industry. For this purpose, there is some advantage if they are fairly distant in time. The international mission of the church now provides us with a similar availability of texts from sources which are fairly distant geographically. What use are we going to make of this material? Some Latin-American theologians are already worried about the danger of their work being treated as a new 'consumer good' in Western circles. The same could now happen to some South African Black Theology — in spite of the dismal lack of interest in Basil Moore's classic collection of essays on this theme when it was published in 1973.[7] A poor church — such as a church-in-mission is almost bound to be — cannot afford the luxury of producing publications primarily for the self interest of the producing industry. New publications will appear only if someone has been satisfied that they will serve a specific functional need. Those who study such texts will miss the point of them unless they are themselves committed to the authors' enthusiasms and priorities. Otherwise, they will be like someone producing an analysis of, for instance, a contraption made out of wood and string and glue and varnish, without any reference to the functional purpose for which it was designed, namely the game of tennis.

A good deal of detailed analysis has been made of Christian texts, especially of the Bible, which is splendidly erudite but betrays no interest in the game for which the makers designed them. Only a tennis-player can really understand a tennis racket. Only a missionary can really understand the New Testament. The missionary will see the material as the original authors did, as a resource for a church-in-mission. In no way will this reduce the need for intellectual rigour and honesty: but it will give her or him the inside view, the identity of interest, without which the resource cannot be understood functionally. And, in case this sounds like a cavalier dismissal of modern scholarship, I would affirm that the greatest single gift of modern New Testament studies has been to create for us some awareness of the context in which the New Testament documents appeared and the ways in which they were resources for churches-in-mission. When we have some identity of interest with a minority, persecuted, insecure, crucified church, puzzled about the criteria for its membership and the future of its work, then we are alongside our comrades in discipleship who produced these documents for their own purposes; and we prove the value of this material functionally.

A missionary movement will be something of a misfit within the ordinary institutions of both church and university. It will be indebted to both and it will be critical of both. It will be critical of the Church insofar as the church fails to embody the truth as disclosed by the living Christ. It will continually be reminding the church of its unfinished agenda, particularly the agenda concerned not just with the formulation of truth but its acting out. It will particularly insist that the truth of the incarnate God be acted out in visible, corporate common life; it will take seriously the fact that 'bodily', 'incarnate' and 'corporate' are three ways, from three different linguistic traditions, of saying the same thing.

The Anglican Catholicism of the last 150 years has had an ambiguous attitude to the academic base also. The successors of the Oxford Movement would be perverse if they ignored their point of origin in the academic world. They have rightly stood for intellectual seriousness and the need to appropriate the whole wealth of inherited wisdom and patristic foundation. More precisely, they have also recognized the strategic significance of the academic world as an area of mission, partly because of the need to recognize all honest intellectual enterprise as a form of humble sharing in the work of the creator, and partly because of the influence of the academic community in the total life of a nation. This has certainly been one of English Anglicanism's more valuable exports. Even in situations where they have had no particular establishment prestige, Anglicans tend to have been among the first to see the need for specialist ministries in the academic world. And this has not been primarily to extract converts from an evil or dangerous environment, nor just to secure a supply of graduate ordinands; the primary purpose has been to recognize the importance of the institution itself as a place where Christian insights have a contribution.

At the same time, a church which is motivated by mission will be cautious about the academic claim to be disinterested or value-free. It will recognize that such a claim is a necessary aspect of academic freedom, with an importance which will be obvious to anyone who has seen what can happen when a university becomes merely a servant of a national ideology. But the ideal of a 'value-free' or 'scientific' pursuit of truth can also encourage people to be refugees from the world of struggle and commitment. Christian faith has to insist that the search for truth is not isolated from the needs of those who most need the changes which truth should bring — those for whom the structures and habits of the present order are a lie and a denial of the truth. A church which is motivated by mission will ask in whose interest the university exists; it will try to discover whether its presence is truly to the advantage of the poor or whether it is concerned primarily with the interest of its own minority. Particularly in the area of theology, a church which is inspired with the vision of the Body will ask whether the university's theology is contributing to the power and prestige of an 'expert' class or whether it is contributing to the enabling of the whole people of God.

The Fathers of the Oxford Movement clearly had a passionate interest in values. Their academic commitment did not lead them to claim to be disinterested. They were, undeniably, scholars. But they were also missionary practitioners. They picked up patristic texts not to engage in historical research but because they passionately believed that these texts were relevant and useful for their particular situation. They were like Canon Allchin's abbot friend.

In several conferences and training courses for ministers and lay workers in the last few years, I have started off sessions with questions such as these: In the last year, what elements of Christian doctrine (or of the Bible) have you found most useful, either for guidance and for interpreting your own ministry or in developing your church's policy? What elements have presented most problems or embarrassments for you? My impression is that about half of the members respond with interest to such an invitation, and reflect on their experience in detail; the others feel that the question is unfair, that doctrine is a thing to be learned and understood and communicated, but that it shouldn't be expected to serve a functional purpose. To me, this difference coincides with the difference between a church-in-mission and a church which is satisfied with self-maintenance.

So the test of truth is not just whether it is accurate or internally consistent. The real test is whether it is body-building, whether it enables the Body to cohere together in love for the sake of God's total purpose in the world (Ephesians 4:14—16). The Catholic movement has an instinct for raising this practical question in the context of intellectual discussion. It does not easily allow an academic lecture to replace the liturgical sermon, and it is not satisfied with a programme which treats people as disembodied minds. Therefore, even when it may not appear to be particularly interested in mission in any specific sense, its total way of thought is missionary: and this comes to the surface most obviously in the high value which it places on the imagery of the Body.

4 The Beginning of Mission

As a model or paradigm of the operational functioning of the church, we can take the second chapter of the Acts of the Apostles. From this we can identify three functions of the church. These all involve our two previously stated themes, the theme of transformation and the theme of the Body. These functions can serve as a method of evaluating the operation of a church-in-mission, and they have particular relevance for the sector of church experience which we are concerned with in this study. The rest of the book will largely be shaped around this distinction of functions.

1   Acts 2: 1—13. A function of healing, reconciliation, boundary-breaking; an overthrow of forces that obstruct God's design in creation.

This first phase of the story concerns the process or manner of communication, rather than the message itself. There are at least three features which should be noted by a church-in-mission.

(a)   The potential mission team has met, and is waiting. Their coming together is not due to the work of the Spirit. As the dry bones in Ezekiel 37 come together in obedience to the word of the Lord, and only then the Spirit makes them alive, so here the potential apostles come together in obedience to Jesus, not knowing exactly what to expect. The patient work of obedient structure-making has to come first; then the Spirit breaks in.

(b)   The coming of the Spirit is, in one sense, a reversal, and, in another sense, a fulfilment, of the meaning of the story of the Tower of Babel (Genesis 11:1—9). At the Tower of Babel, language became confused, and persons were divided into language groups between which communication was blocked. At Pentecost, this is put right; communication is enabled, between people of different language-groups. A common message is heard; and this leads not just to common understanding but also to common praise. A Pentecost church will be also a Catholic church, enabling communication between groups who would not otherwise be in communication with each other.

This is what the miracle is about, the enabling of understanding, not the giving of an experience of ecstasy. Throughout the story there is very little reference to emotional or spiritual states. The role of the Spirit of God is not to give people individual spiritual experiences, or even to bring about a shared corporate ecstasy. The miracle of the Spirit is to create new communities. But before this can happen, the communicators have to be given confidence towards each other.

The miracle of Pentecost is not just that people are enabled to understand each other. The people described in the story would all have been able to make some sense of the great international languages of the day; they were all Jews, and were mostly cosmopolitan travellers. At least, they would have been able to understand each other in Hebrew. The point is made, however, with considerable emphasis, that communication comes to them not in the international language of the powerful but in the local languages of family, region and nation. They all heard the wonderful works of God in their mother-tongues, the most native and deeply running symbol-system inherited from parents in children's earliest years of formation. This is the heart of the miracle. Our own language, however small and local, however insignificant in the eyes of the empire-builders and the powerful advertisers, is claimed as a suitable vehicle for the good news. Holiness does not depend on the bending of our utterances, accents and culture to fit the convenience of the powerful. Right at the beginning, therefore, comes a witness which affirms the value of what we already are.

This is obviously educational good sense. William Morgan, the translator of the Bible into Welsh, in 1588, insisted that 'Religion, if it is not taught in the mother-tongue, will lie hidden and unknown.' But his forerunner, William Salusbury, who translated the epistles and gospels thirty years earlier, perhaps saw deeper into the matter with his warning: 'Unless you wish to be worse than animals, insist on getting learning in your own language: and unless you wish to abandon utterly the faith of Christ insist on getting the Holy Scriptures in your own tongue.' In other words, if your learning is limited to what you can learn through someone else's language, where the someone else dictates not only the answers but the questions, you will be losing your human dignity and value. Your faith will not be yours; it will be the faith of the authority which draws up the catechism. You will be a product of 'classroom religion' only.[8]

Those who heard the apostles' words did not only get information about events external to themselves: they also got an assurance of their own value, through the affirming of the language which shaped their basic perceptions.

(c) The other notable element in the process is very similar in implication. Even the communicators themselves are not people of education and prestige. They were not the sort of people who normally had access to the media. Professional scribes in Jerusalem might, if sufficiently motivated, take crash courses in the mother-tongues of Parthia or Elam: but these were Galileans, distinguishable from the educational aristocracy by their regional accent. They were fishermen and suchlike, people of no natural social significance.

So, while the first section of Acts 2 is indeed about communication, it is primarily about healing and transforming. It describes a provocative action of the Holy Spirit to affirm people's value and to bring them into an experience which unites them in their diversity. The

23

provocative action is, therefore, also a judgement and a criticism of the more destructive forms of unification. Babel is indeed reversed: but the salvation-character of Babel is not reversed, that providential aspect of the story which is treasured by small nations and ignored by large ones, namely that God intervenes to overthrow the devices of one single imperial language-group which tries to dominate the world by means of technological wizardry.

2 Acts 2: 14—39. The communication in words.

First, we need to note that this was not a prepared sermon. The biggest difference between the sermons in Acts and the sermons in our churches is not that in those days the preachers were more inspired, more Bible-based or more successful. The biggest difference is that they did not prepare an address with several days' notice, to give to a self-selected congregation in a specially designed building; nor did they have to look around for a theme. Their sermons were extempore responses to immediate questions, out in the open, subject to interruption and confusion. The preacher did not take an initiative; he responded to a question, and the question itself arose out of a provocative action.

Then, the content of the message explains the provocative act. Peter explains that this is an outpouring of the Spirit. This outpouring was foreseen in prophecy, and the prophecy anticipated that such an outpouring would be socially disturbing. No longer will the Spirit be restricted to 'significant' people for special tasks and occasions, as in the Old Testament dispensation. The Spirit now is being shared by the whole community, including the young, the old and the slaves — three groups who get shunted into the margins of society. And the message concerning Jesus makes this more specific. In brief, it affirms that God has given supreme value to a man who has been most conspicuously and deliberately deprived of value, and who has been treated as one of the most undesirable types of human being, a discredited and convicted agitator. And this is not just objective information. *You,* your people and your whole system of human valuing, have been responsible for this treatment of the one whom God chose; you showed that you did not recognize and honour the good deeds of God in your midst. But God is not limited or thwarted by your stupidity or your ill-will. God is giving you the opportunity to recognize that your system of value-judgements has been perverse and evil. You are being given the opportunity to accept that this one who has been rejected by human judgement is given supreme value by divine judgement. So, this proclamation leads to the question: 'What shall we do?' The answer is: Recognize the new opportunity, and take it (repent). If you can accept this sort of leader, join our movement under his authority (be baptized in the name of Jesus, the Messiah). This is a movement which overcomes the disorder of the world by forgiveness, and you can share in it.

3   Acts 2: 40—7. The formation of community.

The provocative action has led to proclamation. The proclamation leads to the forming of community. It is a community which cuts across the old national divisions. It includes representatives of all the nations mentioned earlier; it is a community of what we would now call Africans, Asians and Europeans — in principle, all the known nations, representing all the offspring of Noah and of Adam. It is a community with a shared table, a shared discipline of worship, fellowship, prayer and sacrament. It is a community which expresses itself by developing a community of goods.

But this has to be seen as the third stage. After the healing action comes proclamation: after proclamation, community-formation. These people can form into the new community only because firstly they have all been affirmed in their existing variety, and secondly because they have heard the message of the divine process of transformation and reversal of the world's valuations. The new community is not based on the members' natural bonds with each other, or on previous acquaintance or on their own selection or choice of each other. It is a new community which recognizes and honours their variety; they are the gift of grace to each other.

One further distinction which can be helpful at this point is the distinction between task and maintenance. Service and proclamation are the task-functions of the church; community-formation is its maintenance-function. Both are vital. It is possible for a church to concentrate so much on its community-life that it forgets its purpose within the world; it gets cosy and satisfies itself by enabling members to feel good. It is also possible for a church to be so preoccupied with its tasks that it has no real room for persons who are not obviously useful or busy within the context of the tasks; it will judge all that it does by usefulness. The maintenance-function of the church picks up one of the central implications of the first section of the Pentecost story, that the Spirit of God affirms the value of people irrespective of their outward status, their achievement, or their deserving. The church is always and originally called to be a community of grace: this is essential to its catholicity.

This account of the functions of the church is, of course, not the only possible one. I chose to make use of it in this story because it provides a convenient classification with which to look at the church in practice. But it is inadequate as a total account of the church's operation. In particular, it does not seem to give proper place to worship, which, after all, has been the most obvious point at which the Oxford Movement has enabled renewal. Any consideration of mission must give major consideration to worship. But worship is not a fourth function to be tacked on to the other three. At every point it enables and underlies the other three. To fail to acknowledge this would be to connive in one of the greatest causes of weakness in the church, namely the separating off of function from function, and the isolating of worship as just one among several options. Worship is the fundamental affirmation of the values which underlie all the programme: worship itself is turned into a self-justifying hobby unless the connections are stressed. And the rest of the programme grows weak in motivation unless the underlying values are renewed.

So, in the final chapter, we will consider how worship and spiritual training relate to the whole enterprise.

CONFRONTING
THE POWERS OF EVIL

5   Casting out Demons

The Gospel begins in confrontation with the powers of
darkness. For Mark, Jesus' first actual dialogue is with a
demon. And the other gospels express the same truth in
different ways.

Africa is the continent with the largest growth in
Christian membership in this century. The estimated
Christian population has risen from 1.2 million in 1912
to 90 million in 1970, and the rate of increase continues.
To those who say that Africans accepted the Gospel because
of pressure from their white masters, we have to say, firstly,
that Africans have never been as servile as that would
imply, and, secondly, that the time of real large-scale
expansion of the church has been when the pressure of
white masters has been withdrawn. What has been the
appeal?

It is quite possible to point out a number of elements in
Christian faith which were already present, in principle, in
African traditional religion. We will come back to some of
these later. The congenial elements reflect the general sense
that African traditional religion, like Catholicism, is a
world-affirming rather than a world-escaping way of life.
The word-made-flesh comes as a fulfilment rather than as a
scandal. Part of the reason for the welcome of Christianity
is these points of contact. But part is also due to the
definitely new things which Christianity has brought,
which are truly good news. Different missionaries will have
different stories. I can only testify to the way in which
some elements in our preaching have been received with
rather special appreciation. When this happens, the preacher

discovers that there is more in the message than he or she had realized. There is a new gospel for oneself in one's own message. I would select two such themes.

As it happens, they are the first two stories in Matthew's gospel. The first story is the naming of Jesus. 'Jesus' is the universal name, the new 'Adam'. It is as non-European as it is non-African. It belongs to no exclusive language-group. It represents a faith that is for all. In any liturgy, you can recognize this name even if every other sound is unintelligible. It was particularly precious in the first congregation of Africans in which I was a minister, a congregation consisting of migrant mineworkers representing all the languages of Central and Southern Africa. Later, I was involved in the founding of a new church-building, and for this reason I proposed that it be dedicated as the Church of the Holy Name, a suggestion which was received with great happiness.

The second story is the Epiphany story. The magi, the so-called 'wise men', sorcerers, magicians, astrologers (the only other *magos* in the New Testament is a distinctly shady character), find their way to the cradle of the infant king (Matthew 2: 1–12). Their culture's science enables them on their way. But it is a science of mystery and manipulation, a science which attributes to inanimate objects the power to influence people's fortunes and decisions, a science which battens on credulity and on people's sense that they are controlled by predetermined forces. These practitioners of this science recognize their Lord. They hand over emblems of their trade and tokens of their profit from it. 'From that time all sorcery and every evil spell began to lose their power; the ignorance of wickedness began to vanish away; the overthrow of the ancient dominion was being brought to pass.'[9] Christ brings to an end the old order of magic, superstition, manipulation, secretiveness, sorcery, and the use of intellectual or spiritual power for sectional or partisan ends. And the actual agents of this science of vested interests are themselves the first to acknowledge the Christ! This is the ancient, classic meaning of the story; and it is powerful good news.

Another valued story shows how Christ confronts the demonic forces which take over and occupy a person, and casts them out (Mark 5: 1—20). Here, the man's whole being, his voice, his behaviour, is controlled by demons; and when he is asked to give his name, he answers in terms of a unit of the invading army of occupation, a Legion. No one who is a member of a colonized population can evade the significance of this. Christ drives out the invader and restores the man to his created sanity. And, because of the economic loss that this causes, people ask Christ to go away. I have known Rhodesian whites say, 'Whatever happens, our blacks must never be allowed to hear this story!' Christ brings not a theory about evil or an interpretation of it; he casts it out.

I am not claiming that all this is the peculiar property of the Catholic movement. But Catholicism has usually taken the supernatural order seriously; and it has celebrated the Holy Name. When theologians have tried to persuade us to delete the demons from the gospels, conservative Catholicism has resisted. And support has come from poets and psychiatrists, who know that without such language people may be unable to speak of their sharpest agonies. The question is not whether demons 'exist'; we might as well ask whether neuroses or electrons exist. The question is whether this language helps — by enlarging our awareness, enabling our ability to give an account of our experience, and giving resources and models for our struggle in company with Christ — or whether it hinders — by increasing our sense of helplessness and non-responsibility.

Catholicism takes our corporate identity seriously. In reading the stories of Jesus, a Catholic approach will ask, 'How does the church, the Body of Christ, express this activity of Jesus in corporate action now? Similarly, in reading stories of demons, a Catholic approach will ask, 'How is this demonic force identified and exorcised in our corporate life now?' Catholics who are competent in exorcism assert that, in their experience, demon-possession of individuals is very rare. And we have to acknowledge that the theologians who have tried to delete the demonic from our contemporary Christian witness have done so because they have been horrified by the terribly destructive effects of incompetent exorcism when practised on individuals. Unless we handle the exorcism stories in the gospels in this corporate style, we will find them being claimed by people who want to find in the gospels a licence to get involved in the secret and irrational world of the occult, or who find satisfaction in diagnosing themselves, as individuals, to be possessed by demons. In my experience, this self-diagnosis never accords with the marks of demonic possession as recognized by Jesus. But this is not to deny the reality of our supernatural warfare. There are demonic forces which threaten human beings, and the church is called to recognize and attack them. Every baptism is an exorcism, an attack on the powers of darkness, and every baptized person is enlisted as a member of the exorcising community.

If the church is to take its role as exorciser seriously, it will need to look carefully at the models of exorcism which are to be found in the activity of Jesus. The gospels show a distinction between exorcism and other forms of therapy. Exorcism is always a confrontation with a power which claims, occupies, controls and exploits its victim. In the case of an 'ordinary' illness, the patient is addressed directly, and the healing mandate is always a word of creation, of encouragement, of enabling — 'Your sins are forgiven,' 'Rise and walk,' 'Be opened.' The patient is addressed as a rational responsible being, who has feelings, motives and attitudes, like other people. The overcoming of a demon is a much more violent scene. Commonly, the first indication that a case is one of demon-possession is that the voice of the victim identifies Jesus and proclaims him as an enemy. Jesus addresses the demon directly and casts it out by a kind of spiritual judo, using the demon's own strength to destroy it.

There are several guidelines for a church-in-mission, from these exorcism stories.

1   It is the enemy of God, rather than the potential ally,

who first recognizes and identifies the agent of God (Mark 1:24).

2   Jesus has the great sensitivity to identify and attack the demon with vigour and aggressiveness, while at the same time identifying and supporting the demon's victim with patience and compassion.

3   Jesus, as we have already noted, distinguishes between occasions where the first move must be caring and support-ive and occasions where the first move must be aggressive and challenging. There are times when the gospel word must be 'Your sins are forgiven'. But to approach a demon with a word of forgiveness is to placate and tolerate the powers of evil and to connive in the continued exploitation of their victim.

4   The fact that a demon-possessed person can break his own chains does not mean that he can organize his own freedom. Freedom comes as a gift, in encounter with a new power, not just by the perfection of one's own muscle.

5   Jesus avoids questions of guilt and blame in cases of demon-possession. The victim is not treated as a sinner. Demons are irrational and their choice of victims is for-tuitous. To treat a victim of a demon as a guilty person is to transfer the exorcist's own frustrations onto an already burdened person.

6   There is often a question of cost. Evil doesn't just go away as a result of some nice people having nice thoughts. Exorcism disturbs the patterns of society and causes loss of value of one kind or another. There are various invest-ments in the continued operation of demons, and any breakdown of the demonic power is against the interests of those who have made such investment (compare Acts 16:16ff). Is one man's sanity worth two thousand pigs? The general public says, No, and asks Jesus to leave.

7   There is a very strong caution in the gospels concerning publicity. Only in really exceptional circumstances did Jesus ask for any advertisement for his healing and exorcis-

ing work. It was not intended as a method of promoting his message. He positively discouraged the sort of publicity which would attract clients. This work was an essential element of the Kingdom which he brought, because the rule of Satan could not be allowed to continue. But the role of public wonder-worker was incompatible with being the bringer of the Kingdom.

8   Lying behind most of these distinctions is a skill in discernment and a sheer purity of action. There is a power of God, a power of the creator, which is able to master the powers of darkness. But it doesn't work automatically. The agent of God needs the dicipline of spirit to see with God's eye, to care with God's heart, and to act with God's power. Confrontation with the powers of darkness needs prayer and fasting; it is not an easy option for the ambitious, the hasty, the egocentric self-publicist (Mark 9:29).

Christ and his apostles were good news. But this was not merely good news for people who like to have a discussion about the origin of evil; they brought good news for people who were in hell and who urgently needed deliverance. The church is called to continue to embody the divine aggression against that which distorts human life and threatens to wreck creation. Catholicism, with its instinct for the realities of supernatural warfare, should have much to contribute to this programme. It certainly does not have any monoply of insight or commitment in the battles against social evil. It has, indeed, at times been thoroughly inward-looking. Although people like Huddleston and the Berrigans base their social commitment on their Catholic faith, perhaps we have to acknowledge that they make their appeal because they are a bit exceptional; the attack on social evil has, as often as not, come from Quakers and Unitarians and others who would not find themselves normally sharing in the Catholic sacraments. None the less, there is logic which does lead from Catholic belief to social witness, and it is not confined to a few eccentrics. It is a logic based on a recognition of the significance of corporate life and of the power of symbols to hold people's imaginations and motives. Fear of evil spirits and fear of sorcery manifest themselves in individuals, but in principle they are fears based in a whole system of fear which claims and exploits whole groups and nations.

The attack on this fear, casting it out, replacing it by the open and non-secretive mystery of the Christian altar and establishing of a community of trust and healing — all this is an exorcism, whether we choose to use the word or not; and it is this which, in spite of many faults and failures, has attracted Africa to Christ.

Similarly, there are millions who are now victims of racism: I do not mean the victims of policies of low wages, migratory labour, and racial injustice. I mean those whose minds are so attuned to the racist lies that they cannot see the truth either about themselves or those whom they oppress. You can no more blame a young white man growing up in the Orange Free State for thinking that blacks are inferior than you can blame the man in the Gadarene grave-yard for talking with the voice of Legion. But that does not mean that you fold your arms and say, 'It's hopeless.' Like Jesus, you attack the demon and cherish the demon's victim. This may look, to the rigid followers of political ideology, to involve compromise and blurred edges. Perhaps. But the use of demon-possession as a political and thera-peutic model can save us from the propensity of some political activists to see everything in terms of blame and guilt. A moral intensity which insists on locating guilt, especially on maximizing the guilt of one's ideological adversary, is in a literal sense satanic; it positively depends on the enemy being as bad as possible, and therefore one sets oneself up in business to be a tempter. So those who try to solve problems by means of this sort of moralism themselves become victims of a kind of ideological demon.

One of the most convincing elements in Ambrose Reeves' campaign against apartheid was his conviction that the campaign was essential for the well-being of the whites. 'I have no doubt,' he maintained, 'that while the immediate effects of compulsory segregation may be felt more harshly by Africans, in the long run it will be the Europeans who suffer most: why? Because no people can continue to inflict injustice on others without grave moral and spiritual consequences to themselves. So it is that when we speak of justice in South Africa we are concerned as much with the welfare of the Europeans as the Africans.'[10]

Reeves saw that the whites themselves were the primary victims of racial ideology. I expect that many blacks would find this point of view something of a luxury, in their more immediate experience of poverty and oppression. But Reeves's judgement at this point does not excuse injustice or make it more tolerable. It does not reduce our commitment to expose and attack what is evil. What it does do is to hold open the wider ranges of truth, so that in opposing the lie we do not become slaves of another lie, and in opposing injustice we do not become agents of another injustice. And in this sort of discernment, the traditional language of demon-possession may have useful relevance.

The Church, as the Body of Christ, continues and extends the incarnation of Christ, not only the compassion and the teaching work of Christ but also his aggression. We have just noted one example of this within the inheritance of the Tractarians, Ambrose Reeves' relentless efforts to expose and attack the destructiveness of apartheid. An earlier example would be the struggle of Bishop Frank Weston of Zanzibar against the forced labour system in East Africa in the years following the First World War. Here was an almost classic case, where an occupying power was using the local inhabitants entirely for its own purposes, as virtually slave labour, and was denying them a voice of their own. Weston's most vigorous anger was directed not at the colonialists themselves but at compromising church-men, whose attempts to interpret the situation were used to make the system acceptable rather than to abolish it.[11] And Weston was concerned not only about Africa. Many missionaries have been passionately concerned to draw the attention of the British public to the great needs of their work-areas overseas, and this has often given the impression that all the problems are over there and all the resources are here. Not so with Frank Weston. After all his work in Africa, probably his best-remembered moment was when he directed the members of the 1923 Anglo-Catholic Congress to attend to the poverty all round them in Britain:

If you are prepared to fight for the right of adoring Jesus in His Blessed Sacrament, then, when you come out from before your tabernacles, you must walk with Christ through the streets of this country, and find the same Christ in the peoples of your towns and villages. You cannot claim to worship Jesus in the tabernacle if you do not pity Jesus in the slum. It is madness to suppose that you can worship Jesus in the Sacrament and Jesus on the throne of glory when you are sweating Him in the bodies and souls of his children.'[12]

Catholic faith had given the bishop the instinct to affirm the true presence of Christ in the world; Africa had enlarged his understanding of the mode of that presence in the poor and neglected. He brought these two influences together in the need to confront the immediate form of madness which was most urgent in his homeland.

In the days of great industrial expansion during Victoria's reign, Pusey was making similar connections: 'If in our eager haste to heap more comfort to ourselves we beat down the wages of the poor, what else do we do than defraud Christ?'[13] This kind of attack on covetousness and competitiveness was, for Pusey, a regular part of the preacher's duty.

There is a common tradition, therefore, to be found in the witness of these representatives of the Catholic movement, in very varying situations. These people put their own reputation, and the reputations of their institutions, at risk by speaking up in Christ's name on behalf of those who have little or no voice of their own. They not only talk about the poor; their habit of affirming the real presence of Christ in the world makes them actually recognize Christ in the poor. I suggest that we can see these examples as applications within new contexts of Christ's ministry of exorcism.

We may perhaps object that Christ and his first apostles successfully cast out devils, whereas the devils that these modern apostles attack seem to be still thriving. Denunciation is no substitute for victory. Here we have to recognize that exorcism is not just a matter of powerful words. Weston, for instance, backed up his public attacks on forced labour with patient political action, which eventually brought success. The leadership of Reeves and his allies contributed to the establishing of the Programme to Combat Racism, which took the World Council of Churches and its member churches deep into controversy. Whatever faults may be detected in detail about the operation of that programme, its main threat was simply this: in a situation where almost all the existing alliances favoured the powerful, it offered a contribution of power to those who had little power, and enabled their voice to be heard. Even in Mozambique, where the new regime has not been friendly to the church, you will not find a church leader who hankers after the old days. The Programme to Combat Racism has contributed to the casting out of something evil; it has had something of the character of an exorcism.

But this has to be balanced against other features in the church's total operation. Both in Mozambique and Zimbabwe, the previous alliances of the church with the oppressor have certainly reduced the church's credibility as a contributor to the building of a healthy society after the great change. South Africa now is waiting for its great change, which will come painfully and with many stops and starts. When change comes, many blacks will undoubtedly remember the names of Huddleston, Reeves, de Blank, Winter, ffrench-Beytagh and many others. More significantly, they will remember names like Tambo, Biko, and Tutu, people of their own identity whose heroic faith and spiritual formation have been affected by the sense that, in one way or another, they stand within the Christian tradition that we are considering. But will these people be remembered as exceptional individuals or as

37

representatives of a whole caring and exorcising church? The memory of a few courageous individuals will serve to make the notion of God more congenial to the newly-free; but it will not guarantee that the church will be allowed a place in the new design. And this is not just a matter of the church's domestic self-interest. In any time of great change, there is the danger of new demons entering an empty house; and the church has always a task, if it is allowed to fulfil it, of reminding the state of its unfinished agenda. The most important question for British Christians and missionary agencies to face now, with regard to South Africa, is: what action of ours now will do most to commend the value of the Christian movement to those who, in twenty years' time, will have most influence within South Africa? It is in these terms that we should make our decisions about investment policies, the sending of expatriate missionaries, the development of the Programme to Combat Racism, and so on. And, from within the Catholic inheritance, we try to make our judgements realistically, on the understanding that this is not just a matter of political manoeuvre in the narrow sense, but a sharing in the supernatural warfare in which our opponents are not specific persons or groups made of flesh and blood, but the great demonic forces which threaten to dominate not only our enemies but our allies and ourselves.

This mandate to confront evil is not a licence for our bad temper or a device to satisfy our need to defeat. The church is in the business of reconciliation and peace-making. But, especially in the last twenty years or so, the question has been coming more and more sharply at us — Where do you have to be in order to make peace? Do you have to be neutral? Can you make reconciliation if you are committed? In the conflicts of the earlier years of this century, a 'Swiss-style' neutrality was possible and useful. But in the black/white and north/south conflicts of the present age, the Swiss are in, on one side, whether they like it or not.

The old heresy of Arianism proposed that Christ could be Saviour and mediator by not being either fully divine or fully human. A Christology for our present needs will have to insist that Christ saves by being divine *and* by being totally committed to being human. Christ is not the external umpire; he is the one who is able to make peace because he is truly representative of the battered and oppressed human community. The human race does not have to rise up, like Prometheus (whom Marx so much admired), to make its claim upon God; God in Christ takes on the role of Prometheus. As the intercessor, Christ cries with the human cry; and at the start of every Mass, the church's *Kyrie eleison* gives voice to humanity's agonizing demand for mercy in a merciless world.

The church is committed to one side in the human struggle; it will have the right to participate in peacemaking not because of the innocency of its neutrality but because of its sharing in the struggle for a new order in a closer approach to the justice of God's kingdom. It will keep its spiritual freedom to be peacemaker, by always insisting that its attack is not directed just at the enemies of the church. Its attack is on that which itself attacks and threatens God's creation. Christ's purpose is to rule the universe with mercy; he comes with his wrath rising against compassionlessness, with his power directed to destroy destructiveness. And this is the mandate to his church in a world where the rich rely on amassing instruments of destructiveness and where the older generation offer to the young an inheritance of redundancy and uselessness and empty days.

The Christian movement is to be sensitive to the presence of evil, but it needs to be careful to avoid labelling things as evil which happen to be uncongenial to its culture or even critical of its institutions. Some critics tend to lump all expatriate church workers together and call them 'the early missionaries' — often meaning people of roughly fifty years ago. These get the blame for the destruction of native culture and institutions; a resulting bitterness has built up into a whole mythology. I have seen something of the unnecessary anguish caused, for instance, by the insistence that Zulu women should abandon their traditional way of arranging their hair. But these missionaries were not all insensitive. The Catholic tradition, in particular, has had an anti-puritan streak in it which has cautioned its supporters against being recklessly critical, negative and destructive. For example, Bishop Lucas of Masasi, sixty years ago, was very sensitively seeking to identify those elements within African traditional custom which could be baptized and incorporated into a Christian discipline and those elements which had to be condemned. In a very thorough list, it is remarkable how relatively small is the second category.[14]

I draw attention to Bishop Lucas's work at this point because, although it would be relevant to other sections of our present study, it fits in best, in my judgement, as an example of the *discernment* which is such a necessary feature of Christ's exorcising ministry. Lucas built this discernment on at least three blocks: first, he really did his homework; he found out about the actual processes of African custom, and he did this in a sensitive and gentle manner. He knew something which too few anthropology research students know, that if you try to analyse a culture on the basis of direct questioning and amassing objective information (even more dangerously attractive in our days because of cameras and tape-recorders), you get information which is distorted by people's resentment at the invasion of their spiritual space. It isn't just royalty that suffers from telephoto lenses. Secondly, he made allowances for the biasses and confusions already disturbing the native culture due to the arrival of a new culture of which he himself was, somewhat unwillingly, a part; he recognized that complete objectivity is not possible in such a situation. So, thirdly, he looked outside his own immediate culture and era for guidance, and found it in the witness of the New Testament and in the decisions of the church during the centuries of missionary endeavour when Europe itself was being evangelized.

This careful discipline of discernment not only saved some harmless practices from unnecessary condemnation and retained useful cultural points of linkage between the familiar and the unfamiliar; perhaps even more important, it saved the agent of change from being identified with destruction for destruction's sake; and it protected both evangelist and evangelized from the old imperialist error, that the people of the culture being evangelized must accept the insignia of the culture which is doing the evangelizing. This, as Lucas realized, is a correct way of understanding the struggle in the New Testament, described in Galatians and Acts 15. Culture is part of creation; language, and other aspects of culture, are, according to Christian doctrine, part of the fulfilment of the divine mandate to the human race in creation. Catholicism always should have a particular knack of avoiding any sense that the Redeemer is polarized against the Creator, and that our salvation consists in being delivered from the effects of the Creator's work.

Ultimately, this discernment rests in the vision that the roles of Creator and Redeemer belong together in the Unity of the Trinity. In practice, it provides the essential skill for any exorcist-community — therefore, any missionary community — which needs to be able to avoid, on the one hand, sailing in and attacking everything which it doesn't happen to like the smell of, and, on the other hand, simply and complacently allowing destructive and evil powers to flourish without challenge. Missionaries have to be especially careful of condemning things which members of another culture simply enjoy and find sustaining. No issue more sharply distinguishes the genuine exorcist from the person who is driven by a self-regarding resentment and negativity. Nowadays, in some East African areas, there is a demand that within the ordinary educational curriculum in schools there should be some treatment of African traditional religion. To supply this need, government turns to the churches, as a source of honest, serious, and reliable knowledge on the subject. An unusual tribute, we may think, to the church's tradition of discernment in meeting an indigenous culture.

6 An Alternative to the Existing Powers

The Assize Sermon of 1833 was, in style and manner, not much like an exorcism formula. It would seem to be a typical piece of licensed controversy, the kind of controversy which is tolerated from awkward people who keep within the rules. It was, in content, a challenge to some of the assumptions current within the establishment: but it was, after all, a sermon for the Assizes, an impeccably conventional function within the establishment's arrangements. It was, perhaps, a specimen of one of Anglicanism's most useful skills — a skill which rightly makes it the envy of more tightly-disciplined bodies like Roman Catholicism and Methodism — namely the skill of containing creative dissidents within the system.

But even the Assize Sermon was raising the fundamental question for a prophetic movement: Can there be an alternative voice within the power-system of the world; is this the calling of the church, and, if so, how does the church fulfill this calling? That could, perfectly well, be the murmuring of a power-hungry ecclesiastical elite. But at least part of the reasoning was that those who held the power in the state could not be trusted to control the church according to the will of God, and that the church was in business to serve a wider range of interests than that represented by those who had climbed to power in the state.

The Tractarian leaders were moved by a sensitivity to the needs of those who got little advantage from the system as it existed. In days of railway engineers and philanthropists, men who had great schemes and drove them on by power of money, muscle, and steam, Keble and Newman and Pusey were people who were humanely and personally concerned for the poor. They saw that such a concern could not stop at helping the poor: it had to attack the acquisitiveness, competitiveness and carelessness of the rich, and Newman insisted that 'the church was formed for the express purpose of interfering or (as irreligious men would say) meddling with the world'.[15] Without benefit of Marxist teaching or of the social insight of the later trade unions, Pusey was able to expose the process whereby the poor were made poor by being deprived of an excessive proportion of the wealth which they created by their labour.[16]

This does not amount to an exorcism of the industrial process: but the Tractarians were able at least to start a diagnosis; and this depended in part on their sense that the church could be independent of the secular power, and on their awareness that people's situations are shaped by the corporate structures in which they are placed and not just by their individual choices. Both of these concerns have been central to the Catholic movement's witness, and have been of great importance in moving out into overseas mission.

We must acknowledge that there is a considerable contradiction within Catholicism at this point. Catholicism claims to teach a great respect for authority. The Tractarians saw liberalism and secularism as subversive of authority and therefore needing to be attacked. Well, the great Old Testament prophets also were conservative figures, upholding the traditional law of God against novel apostacies which favoured the rich and the power bearers and betrayed the interests of the poor. To do this means making a clear distinction between the supreme authority of God and human authority-systems. As long as the two are easily distinguishable, this kind of teaching serves the interests of the Kingdom of God. It is fairly easy to retain this distinction, when one is under a hostile government. But it becomes more difficult when the government is reasonably sympathetic, and when one depends on it for land-rights and security; and it becomes almost impossible when the authority-system is the church itself. Anglican Catholicism has taught a high doctrine of the authority of the church and of bishops, and then has been notoriously selective in telling us which bishops to approve of.

In England, the Anglo-Catholic tradition, more often than not, has been self-consciously anti-establishment within the church. For some, this has channelled and contained their critical and aggressive faculties within the ecclesiastical scene: for others, the ecclesiastical battleground has been a scene within which to develop those critical and aggressive faculties for use in the wider world. So, some Anglo-Catholics have been conformist and uncritical in political and social affairs: others, sharing the same religious viewpoint, have been committed to a positive struggle on behalf of the poor.

These distinctions were taken into new contexts overseas. There have been several areas overseas where the Anglican Church has been developed totally and without compromise in accord with Catholic principles and practice. Anglo-Catholic missionaries have gone to such areas partly to find a place where their religious discipline could be followed without dilution, where their type of Anglicanism could reign undisputed. But this has not meant that the critical and aggressive faculties of these Catholics were necessarily allowed to atrophy. People like Weston, Huddleston and Reeves would probably say that the absence of serious conflict in the area usually called 'churchmanship' released them to fight on the issues that really mattered, the struggle for a just society and for the deliverance of the oppressed.

In South Africa, for a long time, the Anglican Church has been very distinct and distant from the political establishment. The politically aggressive element in the church leadership brought in attitudes and skills from English sources, and had to learn how to use them in public debate rather than within the more secretive systems of the establishment. The politically conformist element has satisfied itself by being a harmless sect with ritualistic trappings — very much as if it were in England but with less prestige. The most significant difference, however, is that the politi-

44

cally aggressive element has seen as its most important target the whole institution of *apartheid*; it has thrown itself into opposing the whole South African establishment ideology which insists that there should be 'no equalization as between black and white in either church or state'. Consequently, the element which I have called politically conformist has accepted segregation and is therefore a whites-only phenomenon. The politically aggressive element has insisted on being non-racial or multi-racial, in defiance of law and custom; it has, perhaps, given higher value to this concern than to the direct care for the poor and the oppressed. Therefore, the kind of white Anglican that blacks have been able to observe most closely has been the Anglo-Catholic of the politically aggressive kind. They know that the kind of Anglicanism that they have learned is also the kind practised by people like Reeves, Huddleston and Winter. They know that other kinds of white Anglicans exist, but they don't expect such Anglicans to take a personal interest in them.

South Africa is a particularly interesting place for observing the operation of Anglican Catholicism outside England: nowhere else in the world is there a situation which combines a strong and permanent element of British origin with a majority element which belongs to a totally different culture: Anglican principles require that, at least at national and regional level, the members of these diverse cultures be held together in a single ecclesiastical structure: and it is a situation where Anglicanism has a significant place within the area's total history and yet is very definitely not an establishment-church.

Just to the north, there is an interesting contrast. In the former Rhodesia, there were several of the same ingredients as in South Africa. There was a minority white population with voting rights, controlling a majority of largely unenfranchised blacks. There was roughly similar legislation governing land-tenure and education. And the Anglicanism which came to Rhodesia was from almost exactly the same stable as that which came to South Africa. There were two important differences.

One difference was that Rhodesia did not have in its midst the great moral and intellectual power of Afrikanerdom, which has held most of the initiatives, for better or worse, in South Africa for the best part of a century. This may seem a strange comment, in view of the notorious fact that Afrikanerdom is operating the most conspicuous example of organised racial cruelty on the face of the earth. But, like other nations which have suffered defeat on their own soil, Afrikanerdom has a profound moral consciousness which either gets wasted on trivialities or else is available for the pursuit of a radical justice. Afrikanerdom was born in dissent and in the search for freedom: its present way of treating blacks is in part a reaction to the way in which it was itself treated a century ago by British power-interests. South Africa would be immensely poorer without the kind of intellectual and moral seriousness represented by, for instance, the Afrikaans-medium University of Stellenbosch. And it was just this element which was absent in Rhodesia. Compared with white South Africa, white Rhodesia was a simple consumer society, morally and intellectually almost illiterate.

The second difference from South Africa was that the Rhodesian political establishment was English-speaking, and that therefore Anglicanism was far closer to being an informal established church than its sister-church in South Africa. There was a handful of creative church-leaders of the politically aggressive type, such as Bishop Kenneth Skelton of Matabeleland, but they seemed to be far more lonely than their brothers further south. One reason for this was, surely, that a church which has some pretensions to being an established church has subtle and deep-running lines of communication with government, which it will not wish to put at risk. There are hot-lines, which, in the case of the British colonies, have depended on a sense that the ecclesiastical and political authorities share a language and social assumptions based on the dominances traditional in England. This was true of the Anglican Church in Rhodesia; there were hot-lines, which, even in times of protest, were still worth keeping warm. But, in South Africa, the lines between the Anglican Church and the political authorities have never been anything but icy for decades.

Zimbabwe is now, suddenly, an ex-colony. It has a completely new political leadership, and the church has a largely new team of bishops. The present bishops are, doubtless, much more sympathetic to the present government than the previous bishops were to the previous government; but the Anglican Church, as such, no longer has any particular hot-lines or affinities with the political authorities. It has suddenly had to learn how to be non-established. It also has the added problem, particularly for its black members, that some conspicuous white Anglicans were notorious for their support for the Smith regime: black Anglicans have to cope with the accusation that their church was on the wrong side.

I have considered it right to go into some detail about this Central African experience, not only because it is of intrinsic interest as a piece of recent history but also because the contrast between Rhodesia and South Africa has particular implications for an evaluation of the Anglican Catholic inheritance.

Tractarianism was born in a moment of protest, and the movement has always depended on a sort of consecrated aggressiveness. The Oxford Movement, in its earliest stage, was a voice of protest against the assumption that the church was just a sector of the secular state. It was a claim for the autonomy of the church as an agent of the sovereign God. There are those who claim that disestablishment of the Church of England remains the main item of the Tractarians' unfinished agenda. This is not my direct concern in this book. What is surely true is that the Tractarians pioneered the necessary original thought and political action to make disestablishment a live possibility for Anglicans. This has not yet come about in England, and may indeed be a somewhat secondary issue even in England – I am not competent to argue the point. What is totally clear is that Anglicanism had to come to terms with the issues involved before it could operate authentically in most situations outside England.

47

I am aware that I have, perhaps incongruously, chosen to reflect on this issue of establishment in the context of the church's confrontation with the powers of darkness. The reason is not that I believe that the establishment is itself the powers of darkness, but that, for better or worse, the church's relationship with the establishment greatly affects its ability to recognize and to attack the powers of darkness.

When Bishop Latimer used the occasion of a court sermon to attack the covetousness of the landlord class, he was using an opportunity which only an establishment role could offer: the church was the only mechanism in sixteenth-century England which could give a son of a yeoman farmer a voice to which the king's conscience could not refuse a hearing.[17] That Elisha-style role is of great value in a church's prophetic witness, and should not be despised. But there is a cost. Balaam may find it very hard to resist being co-opted into the value-system of Balak. Or (notice how this theme crops up in many strands of the Old Testament) Ezra has to look very carefully at the colour of the horses before deciding whether to accept a military escort. (See 2 Kings 6; Numbers 22—4; Ezra 8.)

We affirm that Jesus took on the role of a servant: but he was not the servant of the world in the sense of fulfilling the world's demands and ambitions. He had an agenda of his own. He was not constantly at everyone's beck and call. 'Everybody here wants you — there's lots that needs to be done,' say the disciples: 'Let's go somewhere else, then,' Jesus answers. Nowhere, I think, in the gospels does Jesus give a straight answer to a straight question. Even in healing, he frequently gives people what he knows they need rather than what they feel they want. He maintains an independence; and so must his Body, the Church. It is the Devil, not the divine law, which suggests that you can get political results by making acts of worship. (See Mark 1:37ff; Matthew 4:9.)

For the Oxford Fathers, the sovereignty of the church was not just a political aim; it was a part of the Gospel of salvation for the world. Many who were shaped by this tradition went out from Britain with an ability to see that the Anglican Church could properly and authentically exist without having a formal establishment character.

Bishop Gray, who landed in South Africa in 1848 to be the first Bishop of Cape Town, saw this. He set himself to work within his diocese as if it were a voluntary society and not under the authority of the Colonial Office; and over the next thirty years, after much painful litigation, he proved his understanding to be legally correct.[18] The only form of Anglicanism in South Africa to refuse this identity is the extreme protestant breakaway group calling itself the Church of England in South Africa: it has claimed to be the true representative of the English established church and of the Archbishop of Canterbury (who has had to disown it). It is treated with more respect than its tiny size would suggest; it is the only so-called 'English-medium' church which has consistently supported the South African government and repudiated the World Council of Churches. Its reward came when its bishop was the only non-Afrikaans-speaking church leader to officiate in the funeral of the assassinated Prime Minister, Hendrik Verwoerd.

Bishop Selwyn went to New Zealand with the same outlook as Bishop Gray; he achieved his aims with much less opposition. He established synodical government of the church there as an autonomous body: and in the strength of his experience there, he returned to the Church of England to pioneer lay representation in the councils of the Diocese of Lichfield.

In Wales, 'the old mother', the Church of England, was seriously weakened in its witness by the sense that it was an alien church, a church of the English landlord class. The Oxford Movement moved into Wales to a considerable extent on the wing of the Welsh language; Welsh-speaking Tractarians did much to counteract the alienation of Anglicanism from the culture of ordinary Welsh people. And the church in Wales has found itself freer to be a church for the nation since it ceased to be an established church.

Perhaps the most important implication of all this process is that perceived by W. E. Gladstone; he was himself influenced by the Tractarians, he was politically interested in the disestablishment of the Anglican Church in Ireland and Wales, and he was Prime Minister at the time when the Privy Council declared that the Anglican Church in South Africa was a voluntary society having no legal identity with the Church of England. For him, one of the great lessons of the case of the Church in South Africa was the 'dispelling of the dangerous and mischievous idea which undoubtedly weighs upon the minds of many of this country . . . that when you take away the legal sanction from spiritual things, then spiritual things lose all their force and vitality'.[19]

The force of Mr Gladstone's warning applies in any establishment context. If religion does depend on legal sanction, then what is important in religion must be what is felt to be important by those who have acquired the power to make the law, the secular power-bearers. So religion can become a kind of spiritual police, operating in the interest of the authorities. In that case, it will probably fail to be good news to the poor — which is the decisive question for the followers of Jesus. It is no use having Good News unless we ask, Good News for *whom*? A church which is overtly a device for congratulating the powerful on being powerful will have its work cut out to persuade the powerless that it can be on their side also.

This is the predicament for the white-based churches in South Africa. Even if, as in the case of the Anglican Church, a majority are black, and even if the church is well-known as a critic of government, when white leaders protest against bad laws they are inevitably contributing to the greatest of all South African fallacies, namely that politics is a matter of white people arguing with white people about black people.

Missionary activity in the last 150 years has largely been initiated from churches in Europe which have been establishment churches (even if not formally established churches), churches which have participated in the dominant systems of culture and power in their homelands. Mission has often been an attempt to set up replicas of these churches in new areas; this has operated as a cultural and educational programme, aimed at creating a church which could work with the colonial government in much the same manner as the church in the home country worked with the home government. This was often inevitable and not entirely undesirable. But there were always dangers. There was the danger of setting up an institution to bring a church into being, rather than letting a church grow, and so allowing it to create such institutions as it really needed. There was also the danger of substituting education for conversion; there was the danger that the institutions could be used as hostages by government (some Indian critics allege that the lack of Indian church reaction to the Emergency in 1977 was due to the vulnerability of their institutions, and the same has been true of mission schools in South Africa). Above all, there was the danger of the church becoming a kind of 'national church', inhibited from exercising a ministry of corporate exorcism and from identifying the public forces that oppose the Kingdom of God. Is there a national church which has ever offically condemned its nation for going to war?

That quasi-establishment role has disappeared in many places. The change which came to the Anglican Church in Zimbabwe has been typical, and the Anglican Church elsewhere exists in a very wide variety of ways in relation to the rest of society. It exists in places where it once was at ease with the state and has suddenly learned how to be a confessing church — as in Uganda; it exists in places where it has had to live without external communications — as in Burma; it exists in places where it has no obvious cultural reason to exist at all, such as Madagascar or Uruguay; it exists in places where it retains a certain historic dignity but with no particular prestige or connection with secular leadership — as in Australia, or Scotland.

From the experience of these churches, we can see that to be non-established does not guarantee a closer obedience to Christ. The strongest argument in favour of establishment is that it keeps the church in a bonded responsibility to the secular world, of the kind which Bishop Latimer well exploited. The greatest danger for a non-established church is that it can become *merely* a voluntary society, an individualistic and egocentric hobby which absorbs its laity so greedily into its domestic preoccupations that they have neither the time nor the will to exercise their spiritual muscle within the secular world. The nearer the church gets to becoming a sect, the more it is in danger of extracting lay people from their mission in the world and absorbing them into the organization of the church. Synodical government may be good for the church; but, like any other activity of the church, it has eventually to be judged by whether it enables or discourages people in the exercise of their abilities on behalf of God's Kingdom in the world. This is, I would think, one of the most useful questions which could be put to any Partnership-in-Mission consultation between members of different provinces of the Anglican Communion.

Anglican Catholicism has had its share in the processes which I have been describing, and has certainly not been spared the dangers. A ritualist kind of religion, whatever may be its ecclesiological theory, can quite easily acquire the character of a sect; apart from anything else, it is a rather expensive kind of religion, and can absorb a lot of resources. But the tradition of Catholic Anglicanism did move into overseas mission with certain advantages, of which the most important was its experience of being already a critical minority within an established church.

Establishment, of course, is far more than a matter of church—state relations. It is the essential issue whenever the church seeks to have an existence within the secular world. It is not only a matter of bishops in the House of Lords, or of mayors' chaplains. It affects, for instance, every chaplaincy in industry, or in the medical services, or in tertiary education.

'Chaplaincy' can mean a provision whereby the church serves people whoever they are and wherever they are,

52

giving them its ministry regardless of whether they are contributing to the inequalities and divisions of society, or whether they are suffering under these evils. 'Chaplaincy' can then be a kind of spiritual welfare service; quite often this is what the institutions seem to want and sometimes are willing to pay for. The alternative policy, which evangelicalism usually finds more attractive, is to regard the institution as fairly irrelevant, and to take people *out of* the secular *into* a religious home-ground — the local church or chapel — and send them back in a renewed condition.

If the first style can be called 'colonial', the second can be called 'extractive'. Neither is truly incarnational. To be true to the style of Jesus, the Body of Christ has to belong truly *within* the world's institutions. Sometimes, with caution, it may come in at the invitation of management; sometimes, with a different sort of caution, it may claim the Easter-night role of Christ the burglar, and work its way in despite bolts and bars. There are plenty of examples of both, for instance within higher education chaplaincy work in Britain. But, having got there, the Body of Christ has to be critic as well as consecrator, exorciser as well as comforter, aggressor as well as counsellor. And this is what a Catholic sensitivity is all about.

7 Mission and Healing

For much of the period we are considering, the last 150 years, Anglicanism as a whole had little awareness of a ministry of healing. This lack of interest, in which the Catholic movement has shared, has had the effect of making those who have gifts of healing appear to be cranky and unworthy of serious attention. This has coincided with the tendency of British culture to develop specialist institutions for looking after different facets of life. Those who come from the contemporary 'Third World' tend both to admire the singlemindedness of these specialisms and to warn, very correctly, of the danger of compartmentalization, of thinking that you solve problems by attending to them in detachment from the complex social environment which really shapes people. Christian enthusiasts have put great energy into this kind of specialization, not least in the sphere of healing.

More recently, many Christians of all kinds have started to insist that healing is part of the essential calling of the church and part of our total obedience to the Gospel. There are four attitudes which Catholicism has brought to this matter. Firstly, Catholicism is always a bit suspicious of compartmentalization. It seeks to see life whole and to see a person whole. It is suspicious of tendencies to detach specialist interests from the common life of the total body corporate of the church. Also, it is suspicious of a view of the human person which assumes that there are rigid boundaries between body, mind and spirit, both in sickness and in health.

Secondly, Catholicism has never relaxed its commitment to the sacramental system. For a time, it allowed the sacrament of anointing to be seen only as an immediate preparation for death: but it was not completely able to disguise the fact that this was a deviation from the ancient purpose of unction as a sacrament of healing. More generally, Catholicism has encouraged people to see the activity of God in physical signs and visible rites; such ceremonies as the laying-on-of-hands fit naturally into such a tradition.

Thirdly, Catholicism has always seen ministry as corporate, not individualistic; it insists that the activity of God does not primarily depend on the worthiness or skill of the minister. It tends to emphasize the impersonal character of the minister. (A priest has his own private cassock and surplice, but at the Eucharist he uses the vestments which are used in common by all the priests of that particular church; in a racially sensitive area, in a church where vestments are normally used, people naturally think that if a white priest prefers to use cassock and surplice, the reason is that he doesn't want to wear the clothes which have been worn by a black priest. This deduction may not always be correct, but its logic is quite clear, and it depends on a feeling that at this point a priest ought to be to some extent impersonal, sharing in a common role with common insignia.) Catholicism tends to distrust highly individualistic kinds of ministry, and therefore, has been suspicious of the kind of healing ministry which depends on star personalities.

Fourthly, Catholicism has a bias in favour of that which is open, accessible to all, and emotionally restrained. Sometimes it has been so suspicious of emotion that it has encouraged a dry and calculated anti-emotionalism — failing to recognize that this is, in itself, a type of emotional stance. This has led it to be very dubious, not say hostile, towards a kind of 'healing' which appears to depend on the manipulation of emotional states. At this point, it is entirely true to the New Testament witness: nowhere in the gospels is there any suggestion that emotional uplift is primary evidence for the presence of the Spirit of God.

This distrust of emotionalism is one reason why the Catholic movement has concentrated on the sacramental ministry to the individual, by the provision of the ministry of confession and absolution, the laying-on-of-hands, the anointing, and the reserved sacrament. This has often been in conscious contrast to the more emotionally florid ministries offered elsewhere. This is fine as far as it goes; it has helped to rescue the ministry of healing from the two contrasting dangers of personal eccentricity on the one hand and complete disuse on the other.

But Catholicism's healing ministry has been limited by its privateness. This is, perhaps, an uncharacteristic defect to find in Catholicism: it occurs in spite of Catholicism's own genius for corporateness: it is due more to western individualism than to any coherent ideal in Christian teaching. The difference can be noted by any pastor who has offered this sort of ministry both to white Westerners and to black Africans. I have many times said, at the end of the Eucharist, 'I have reserved some of the sacrament and I'm going now straightaway to take it to Mr or Mrs X who is ill at home; who would like to come with me and represent the fellowship of the church?' With white groups, almost always the feeling has been, 'Illness is a private matter and we don't want to invade someone else's place and cause embarrassment.' With Africans, the problem has been, how to avoid the whole congregation wanting to squeeze itself into a tiny hut or bedroom: they come along and sing and share in the laying-on-of-hands, and one hopes that the patient can in fact cope with it all. The difference lies in the natural corporateness, which is virtually the natural Catholicism of the African way of seeing such things.

'When there is a thorn in the foot, the whole body must stoop to pull it out' — so we learn from a famous Zulu proverb, which is followed by a less famous but still more searching piece of wisdom, 'and you may have to take another thorn to get it out with.' Any church-in-mission would do well to ask itself, 'What, for us, is the second thorn?' 'If one man of our race is ill, we all are ill' is the opening line of a Sekhukhuni herbalist's advertising mandate, which continues immediately to say, 'To any man or woman the essence of life is the bladder,' and offers various treatments for the control of bile. In this kind of world-view, not only can Catholicism be naturally at home; there is a real opportunity for Catholicism to be renewed, and sent back north with new confidence. Above all, Africa at this point has the simple conviction that anything to do with God must have something to do with healing, physical healing, spiritual healing, social healing. This is what its religious ceremonies have traditionally been about. Africa has happily received from the missionaries the novel idea that it's a good thing to have a religious ceremony for no better reason than that Sunday happens to be the first day of the week. But Africa will still insist that a religion which isn't concerned about healing, and is not specific to immediate needs, isn't a religion at all.

There is a shadow side to all this. When a religious enthusiasm fails to keep its eye primarily on the Gospel of God's grace and creative love, it can make the diagnosis and treatment of evil its chief occupation. This can lead to an excessively moralistic interpretation of events, a belief that all misfortune has a cause, a morally identifiable source. This is the most dangerous and unattractive element in the world-view of many Marxists: it makes for limitless self-righteousness, a projection of all evil onto an identifiable enemy. African socialism is fairly suspicious of international communism and seeks to avoid being trapped into any new colonizing. But at this point, there may be the most logical and destructive point of contact between an unsophisticated Marxist world-view and a common African world-view. Both systems have this deep sense of the moral coherence of the universe; both find it very difficult to accept that misfortune may be nobody's particular fault.

Allotting blame is one way of solving the universal human anxiety about the difference between the way things should be and the way things are. The danger is that it leads to that most terrible of all human solutions, both in Europe and in Africa, the witch-hunt. Sorcery is the deliberate attempt to do harm to others by spiritual means: it tends to be secret, and its practitioners operate in secret: their services may often be sought, but no one officially approves of them. The terrifying thing about witch-hunting is that, when it happens, it is seen as necessary to the public good. It is a do-it-yourself salvation. And of course it takes someone competent in the craft of sorcery to track down and destroy someone who is supposed to be guilty of sorcery.

All this is closely relevant to the ministry of healing, if only because the presence of obvious physical misfortune is the natural starting-point for the practice of this deterministic logic. Jesus and the apostles lived in communities which were anxious about the 'why' of such misfortune; they, on the whole, didn't enter the logic of debate but took people into the larger logic of God's enacted and creative love. This is the authentic task of the church. It can show that the treatment of evil can be to heal rather than to blame. And it gives a specific process for this in the context of individual guilt.

8   Mission and Guilt

Catholic Anglicans have insisted on the importance of the sacrament of penance being made available. They have rightly claimed that to publicize and practise this ministry is an essential part of obedience to the Prayer Book and to the mandates of ordination. We cannot evade the basic instruction of Christ, that the apostolic church is in business to forgive sin, and if it fails to act as a forgiving agent there is no other valid source of forgiveness (John 20:23).

In those Anglican dioceses in Asia, Africa and the Caribbean which have been most affected by the Catholic movement, people have been taught that the sacrament of penance is so important to Christian discipleship that it should not be considered optional. Even today, when the discipline is less rigidly advocated, one of the biggest differences for an Anglican priest going from Britain to Central Africa will be the demand made on his time for this ministry in preparation for Lent and the great festivals.

The practice of this sacrament has been linked rather ambiguously with healing. On the one hand, in sickness it is usually linked very closely to the laying-on-of-hands and anointing. On the other hand, the church certainly does not want to give the impression that cleansing from guilt is required only when someone is actually ill. It is necessary also to avoid supporting the assumption that illness is *always* linked to guilt and to inter-personal alienations. African independent churches tend to put great stress on this linkage: they provide rituals for vomiting or spitting out anger and hatred, as part of the ministry of healing. Catholicism is not wrong to be cautious at this point. When we provide for confession and absolution in the context of the specific sacraments of healing, the reason is not that there is necessarily a direct causal link between the sickness and the guilt; the truer reason is that any unacknowledged guilt can act as an obstruction to the flowing of the grace of God.

But Christianity has moved into a society where people expect religion to relate to the natural crises of life. Where the church prescribes religious activities which are not primarily related to these crises, there is a real danger of the activities becoming self-authenticating routines. The priest or catechist tells the church member what activities are sins; and the church member turns up in the confessional, at the proper times in the liturgical year, with a select list of these sins. At the worst, this becomes 'classroom religion', the repeating of a lesson, rather than what the Prayer Book calls 'opening one's grief'. The whole thing can become a routine which obstructs rather than enables the flowing of the grace of God: and the church member may feel the need to go elsewhere to find healing for the really felt alienation.

Perhaps, British Christians will say, there's nothing special in all this: we have the same problems here. The difference, I suggest, is that Africa has a higher expectation that religion will connect to the events, both recurrent and occasional, of the natural order. Catholicism suffers from the strength and coherence of its own programme. It has its cycle of fast and feast, its celebration of the mysteries of redemption. It tends to be suspicious of folk-religion, and to be scornful of such things as harvest festivals. It is theoretically committed to seeing the unity of creation and redemption, but in practice keeps itself to the purity of the celebration of redemption, because this is where it has its own expertize and where its knowledge is under its own control. So it tends to know what people *should* want, what people *should* feel guilty about, and to be a bit reluctant to cope with the fact that people don't all fit so neatly into the system. One of the blessings of engaging in mission in new cultures is that this sort of rigidity becomes more clearly exposed as an obstacle to the Gospel:

a church which overcomes such a problem in its overseas mission should be able to translate the lessons back into its work in its home base.

The main reason, as I have suggested above, for including confession in the context of the healing sacraments is the simple and general one that unacknowledged sin obstructs the free flowing of God's healing grace. This is true not only for the patient but also for those who seek to share in ministry to the patient. Once a group of people get together to pray for a sick person, or to share in the laying-on-of-hands, they need to realize that unforgiven sin in themselves may be just as big an obstruction to grace as unforgiven sin in the patient. We confess our sins not just to cleanse our individual guilt but because we contribute corporately to the obstruction of God's purpose.

Our general confession in church is not just a sum total of the sins of individual members of the congregation: it is the church's corporate acknowledgement that it has failed to be properly the Body of Christ; in its thoughts, words, deeds and omissions, it has not fulfilled its calling.

In its overseas mission, the church has moved into areas which have a natural instinct concerning corporate guilt. There are African tribes and communities, which have regular reconciliation ceremonies, in which there are gifts and sacrifices for both individual and corporate hatreds and other damage. Again, this sort of ceremony has been picked up more by the independent churches than by the main-line Christian denominations. In the West, the practice of individual sacramental confession has been somewhat declining — although within Anglicanism it is less the preserve of a narrowly-defined Anglo-Catholicism than it used to be. Those who lament this 'loss of the sense of sin' need to recognize that it is balanced by a great growth in a sense of corporate guilt. This guilt is largely about the ways in which nations have hurt nations; so it is closely relevant to any concern about international mission. The fact that the responsibility for these hurts cannot be attributed to specific individuals does not ease the problem. People in fact feel corporate guilt (even if they don't use that language): and, like anyone who is motivated by unresolved guilt, we in our groups act with unhelpful and self-regarding responses. We try to shuffle off our guilt, or to punish ourselves, or to organize do-it-yourself atonement schemes, or to project the guilt off onto someone else.

Genuine penitence is very necessary in public and in international affairs, and is difficult to express sincerely. The British monarchy could, perhaps, contribute by acknowledging its involvement in the sin of Ireland: even Christian comment about Afghanistan would be made more realistic if we were willing to ask just what were *we* doing in that country only a few decades ago.

Over two hundred years ago, Lord Thurlow put the realistic question: 'How can you expect a corporation to repent, when it has neither a soul to be damned nor a body to be kicked?' But surely the church is, in a sense, a corporation which already has the equipment for such a corporate repentance. Catholicism, in particular, has, deep in its nature, a skill in bringing Christ's forgiveness to bear on uncomfortable consciences: and it has an instinct for corporateness. In its international mission, it has the opportunity to let these two inheritances nourish each other.

9 Mission and Medicine

We have noted several factors which have made Catholicism somewhat cautious about entering the field of 'spiritual' healing as a specialist ministry. But there has been a simpler and larger factor which has turned the healing instincts of most Christian missions into a different direction. Anglican Catholicism has been developing at a time of massive growth in the scale and competence of scientific medicine. In our present phase, the institutions of scientific medicine are coming in for a good deal of criticism; but, whatever its shortcomings, we are surely right to insist that it is indeed one of God's most wonderful gifts.

When the church has moved into overseas mission, it has, more often than not, been confronted by massive problems of disease. It is one of the more obvious glories of Christian missions, that they have so often seen that their following of Christ means healing as well as preaching. The same mission team has founded church and hospital alongside each other. The irony now is that in these days it is sometimes very difficult to get medical staff who are Christian, and somewhat easier to get medical staff who have no formal Christian commitment but who feel that the mission hospital just makes real sense. Humanists and agnostics see the need, and willingly give themselves in service: they join existing work but they do not seem to have the institutionalizing wit to get work started: that seems still to be a particularly Christian skill.

At this point, more than most, it would be quite wrong to select Anglo-Catholic mission hospitals for special attention, let alone for special praise.

There are two opposite dangers for a Christian hospital:

one is to let the narrowly evangelistic motive dominate the medical motive, and to treat patients as a captive audience for religious exercises: the other is to detach the physical from the spiritual altogether, and to make the hospital a place of purely scientific competence. The first danger has led to considerable distrust of Christian institutions, especially in parts of Asia: the second has led many people, especially in Africa, to feel that they have to go to the hospital for part of their treatment but they have to go secretly to traditional resources for another part. This latter experience is likely to produce a divided self, a fractured person and a dislocated social spirituality.

In the last twenty years or so, many mission hospitals have become more efficient, more hygienic, larger and more clinical. They have also been depending more on short-term staff, who do not have the chance to get under the skin of the local culture and language. In earlier, simpler days, mission hospitals maintained a dual character more easily, with a programme which recognized both the distinctions and the connections between the physical and the spiritual. It was this character which attracted, and still attracts, people to walk twice as far to a shabby mission hospital as to a splendid government hospital. The mission hospital's problem now is how to improve technical standards and at the same time to maintain this dual character.

Another difficulty for the mission hospital is that, by its very nature, it points to the government's unfulfilled agenda. Governments don't much like this. In a South African Bantustan, a government doctor would not dream of stating, 'Cause of death, starvation'. A mission hospital doctor can be more independent both in conscience and in funding; he can make an objective judgement and call starvation 'starvation'. And he can be deported for so doing. This has happened to Anglican mission doctors, among others, and needs to be recognized just as much as the deportation of bishops. Further, a truly Catholic understanding of human relationships can cause a medical superintendent to insist on organizing the common life of the hospital staff on the basis of a medical and a human community, and not on the basis of an artificial and irrelevant system of racial classification. This was the particular contribution of Doctors Margaret and Anthony Barker at the Charles Johnson Memorial Hospital in Zululand. This practical implementation of Christian community drew on them the wrath not only of government but also of the official opposition — an almost sure evidence of heroic sanctity![20] But, in most areas of overseas mission, the mission hospitals have less autonomy than they used to, and in many places they have been taken over by government; missionaries and other expatriates can sometimes work in them, but with no special privileges, and sometimes under definite obligation not do anything which could be called evangelism.

10   Healing in Society

However it may be modified, the Christian tradition in mission overseas has grown to maturity in holding a ministry of healing and service in very close association with its ministries of proclamation and of church-planting. Once one has caught the spirit of this tradition, one tries to see its application in other contexts. Any church-in-mission can do well to ask, 'What, in our situation, corresponds to the mission hospital?' Where is healing needed? Where are there needs which other agencies have neither the insight nor the resources to supply?

For instance, in one almost entirely non-resident university overseas, there were two chaplaincies. Chaplaincy A looked at the problem of the non-resident population of commuting students and decided: 'All our students live very far out from the university, so they have great difficulty in coming together for worship on Sundays, we must organize a transport system for them on Sunday evenings.' Chaplaincy B said: 'All our students live very far out; they spend very little leisure time together so they don't get to know about each others' studies and disciplines and professional enthusiams in the way that students do who live together in residences: we must organize opportunities for positive sharing of ideals and visions, of this kind, during weekday lunch-hours.' The second proposal originated quite consciously with the putting of the question, 'What, in our situation, corresponds to the mission hospital?'

The Christian movement cannot escape its mandate to heal. Healing is an essential part of the apostolic commission. But it does not necessarily involve all the expense of the traditional mission hospital. Mission in the last hundred and fifty years has been, at the institutional level, part of the movement of the rich world towards the poor world. Missionary agencies have acted on the claim of Jesus to offer more abundant life, and they have seen themselves as agents and dispensers of this abundance. They have gone out from the 'developed' world to the 'undeveloped' world, partly, perhaps, with a colonizing motive and partly in a spirit of sheer compassion. We now have to realize that this sort of arrangement is by no means essential to mission. In the mission work of Paul, mission was a movement from the 'poor saints' in Jerusalem towards the more affluent areas of the central Mediterranean. Paul brought no educational or medical institutions, but signs and wonders of healing and liberation accompanied his proclamation. If there were any patterns of dependency in his work, it was a dependency of the evangelizers on the evangelized, not the other way round.

So the mandate to heal and serve does not necessarily involve the maintenance of expensive institutions. Mission agencies need to examine very carefully how far they contribute to the dependency of the 'Third World'. At the end of the so-called 'development decade', the rich nations were richer and the poor nations poorer; and so we have the sort of demands for better distribution, represented by the Brandt Report.[21] At the same time, people in Africa and Asia are seriously criticizing the models of developed-ness offered by the West, not least in connection with healing and public health. The question for the mission agencies now must be not 'How do we, the strong, help them, the weak?' but, 'What action of ours will most enable others to become less dependent on us?'

For instance, missionary societies and other church agencies, quite properly, bring considerable numbers of students to Britain from the 'Third World'. These students, inevitably, make a kind of instant photograph of the Britain that they meet. They are put into our specialist educational institutions: they often live within the more 'desirable' parts of our cities. They see the consumer goods: they do not see the historical cost of producing such goods, in human or environmental terms. So they usually fail to see about three-quarters of what the British experience is really all about.

I recall a valuable conversation with an overseas student who was a priest from Lesotho. He made it clear that he expected to get a lot of sympathy and financial support for his people during his time in Britain. He described vigorously the poverty of the families and the bad working conditions of the migrant workers who had to go off to earn a living on the South African gold mines. I pointed out that, only two generations ago, colliers in Britain were at least as insecure and exploited as black miners in South Africa: and a young priest from South Yorkshire, a child of the coal-field, capped this by saying, 'And what has caused the difference? Not a development agency from six thousand miles away, but the people taking their situation into their own hands and standing together.' After several years' working with students from the poorest countries overseas, I am left with the conviction that the one useful thing we can teach them is something of the history of the British trade union movement.

And this, of course, could be a highly ambiguous lesson. Are we going to offer, as a model of a good society, the sort of achievement which we have in Britain, for instance in higher education, which shows that change does not really affect the shape of society but just incorporates a larger number of people into the existing patterns of domination? Are we going to help with the provision of ladders on which the most active and advantaged members of the poor communities can climb up out of their predicament, leaving most of their friends behind? This pattern, which David Lloyd George operated so successfully, is just what Mordecai warned Esther against (Esther 4:13ff). This is what Jesus, clearly a self-possessed, independent and mobile kind of personality, refused to do. But it is what our Western-based development agencies are accused of doing, often, I have no doubt, unfairly.

Though certain numbers from among the down-trodden have benefited from a variety of projects and reforms, on the whole it is the rich and those with skills who have improved their condition, while the poor and unskilled have become relatively marginal-ised . . . Those who have operated the reforms and the projects have become a new cadre with money and influence, especially due to massive foreign aid. Clergy and laity, including the missionaries, even though working on behalf of the oppressed masses, have become a new elite.[22]

So speaks the Bishop of Kurunagala, Sri Lanka; and he reflects a good deal of disquiet, even among missionary societies, about the effects of development. The agents of healing in apostolic times started from the position, 'Silver and gold have I none.' (Acts 3:6). What they had to offer put them into no alliances with wealth. Healer and healed were on the same level; and those with special privilege had to accept healing on the same terms as any-one else. The Bishop of Kurunagala sees hope in the development of the role of what he calls the 'community agitator' — the person who from within an oppressed community helps people to become aware of their situation and to take corporate action. And he sees the task of missionary societies as including the support and interpret-ation of the work of such people, and perhaps the sponsor-ing of such people within the racial minorities of Britain.

Here we find ourselves again in company with the Oxford Fathers. They realized that, for the restoration of society, something more than an alliance between church and secular power was needed. It will not even be sufficient for us to commit ourselves to development work, if, by 'development' we mean the hope that there will be a general improvement all round so that the poor can have a few more pieces to pick up. The Oxford Fathers pitted their dogma-based realism against the blander world-views on offer.

Social evil has to be accounted for . . . Social evil is either a stage in the realization of the social good, or it is the contradiction of the social good which will not issue in its opposite. If it is the latter, its root is sin, the misdirection of choice. If it is but a preliminary stage of an evolution towards the Good Society, there is no use in Catholics or any other school of thought denouncing it. If it is the effect of sin, no sociology can afford to give to a dogma of sin and redemption other than a central position in its thought.[23]

This uncompromising statement (which, given their understanding of 'sin', Marxists would presumably applaud) takes us towards another role and function of church. For this, the following observation of a secular development officer in Africa may serve as an introduction. This development officer had responsibilities in two neighbouring nations. Both were (and are) very poor. One was cheerful, vigorous, optimistic; in the other, most people were apathetic and only a few were interested in the possibilities of change. In the first area, he was content that development work could go ahead. In the second, he was convinced that development schemes would be picked up only by the minority, and that they would increase the divisions of wealth and social status. 'In that area,' he said, 'no development work can safely be undertaken until the people have been evangelized and have come to accept the implications of the Christian gospel.'

In the foregoing section of this book, I have followed the pattern of some parts of the New Testament, in which the provocative action of healing comes first, and is followed by the proclamation of the Word. This is a right and normal pattern: but it is not rigid. Sometimes the first stage must be the announcement of good news. And to that we must now turn.

PROCLAIMING THE GOOD NEWS

11 The Mission and the Message

The Oxford Movement was profoundly and passionately committed to the Truth. It gave rise, directly or by reaction, to a vast growth of publications: it brought theological controversy back into the public arena in a way which had not been known for centuries.

There was a fundamental purposive question underlying even the more apparently theoretical arguments of the Tractarians. The question could perhaps be expressed as: 'What is it that enables the human being to draw near to God?' The whole programme of education, sacraments, church order, liturgy, art, devotion, morality, centred on this sort of purpose. The Christian church has a duty, a mandate, and equipment, to enable this approach to God. To fulfil its duty, it has to avail itself of all the equipment which God in his merciful wisdom has provided; and it has to keep itself clear from mistaken philosophies and from political alliances which may obscure its purpose.

This was all very laudable. But it did presuppose that basically the church is located within a Christian culture and has to be recalled to its true obedience within that culture. There is no place, within this picture, for primary evangelism. Yet during the following 150 years, followers of this tradition pioneered many areas of primary evangelism, with apostolic charity, theological firmness, and a disciplined self-sacrifice based deeply in the sacrifice of Christ, which is made truly present in our midst by means of the sacrifice of the Mass.

It would be impossible here to go into detail of how Catholic teaching had to be re-expressed in order to be communicated in the context of primary evangelism. All

Christian traditions have had to work out their proclamation in the context of the thought-forms of groups of people who have not previously been influenced by Christian ideas. There has been plenty of disagreement about this, and the lines of disagreement have cut across, rather than along, the traditional denominational boundaries. How does one speak of the great and world-changing miracles of the incarnation in a culture whose stories treat the incarnation of a divine being as an almost commonplace event? How does one speak of the sacrifice and self-giving in the Christian pattern of atonement, in a culture where mercy is given on the painless command of a supreme power-bearer? But we must also ask, how does one speak of Christ as the freedom-bringer in a culture based on the notion of free enterprise, the right of the powerful to be free to take advantage of the less powerful? How does one speak of the Kingdom of God in a culture which holds the political powers at a great distance, a culture in which something wonderful is reckoned to have happened when royalty indulges in a walkabout? There are always problems of this type and they are not confined to primary evangelism. But the experience of others can offer guidelines, encouragement and warnings. Let us consider some reflections based on examples drawn from areas affected by the Catholic tradition in Anglicanism.

Absolutely primary evangelism is, of course, less common now than it was fifty or a hundred years ago. But recently Canon Ronald Wynne has had an opportunity for this sort of work among the Hambukushu people in the far north-west of Botswana. They arrived there in 1967, refugees from the tyranny of the Portuguese administration in Angola. They had had no previous encounter with Christian mission: their language had hardly been written down at all, or learned by people outside their group. This presented the first task to Canon Wynne when he started working there soon afterwards, under the authority of Bishop Kenneth Skelton of Matabeleland: the result of this element in his work is his publication, through the University of Cape Town, of the first Mbukushu dictionary.

There was one feature in the Hambukushu people's experience which helped in making contact with their world-view: they were very much an Exodus people: they had known deliverance, very precisely according to the Exodus pattern. God, who had previously been a very distant being, to be approached only through the ancestors, had come close and had acted decisively for them. The evangelistic task was to help them to work through from a local, Moses-style understanding of the divine purpose to a wider, inter-tribal understanding, on the models of Abraham and Adam. The method was just to go on exchanging stories, offering stories which led to a continual widening of horizons. And this went on for seven years before it became appropriate to speak directly about Jesus and to offer baptism.

One conclusion which Canon Wynne is very convinced about is that, in this sort of situation, one must start with and patiently work with the Old Testament witness; only when the Old Testament connections are established can one move on to the figure of Jesus. The main reason for this is that this order shows the Old Testament as the less mature stage and the New Testament as the more mature. If Christ is brought in first, and Moses later, Moses inevitably is seen as the fulfilment and Christ as the preliminary: the model of Moses displaces the model of Christ. Clearly this is a major matter of evangelical and educational strategy, and not all would agree with it. But the logic is of great importance. Canon Wynne goes so far as to say that, in Africa, it is in the areas where the biblical message has been offered the wrong way round that social change has come about most obviously according to Old Testament norms, by competitive violence rather than by the developing of fundamentally new communities of reconciliation.

A sense of the importance of contact with the ancestors is, of course, important in many parts of Africa. It is particularly important for people who are shunted around and have few political or economic or material possessions to make them feel free and secure. Members of the international cosmopolitan community (and this includes missionaries), who are propelled around the world at other people's expense, have no right to despise this ancestor-consciousness. Far better is it to relate it, as Canon Wynne has done, to the available treasures of Catholic doctrine. He preaches thus:

> When you die, you will be remembered as one of the living dead, and food will be set aside for you by your family, so that after five years you will become one of the nameless multitude of ancestors . . . Christ has been where your living dead and your ancestors are now. He offers them the same hope that he offers to you, that they and you may be with God for ever. Is not this good news?

And Canon Wynne adds: 'Directly I said that, a young African priest with whom I had been talking of these things, rose to his feet and grasped my hands in his and said, "If I were not a Christian this is where I would ask for baptism." '

Is this just a romantic story from far away? Well, apart from anything else, it shows how necessary it is to keep the contents of one's doctrinal tool-kit clean and service-able, even a rusty old spanner like the Descent into Hell. But I have no doubt that this element of Catholic doctrine is important for us in Britain, properly translated. Racism, and destructive types of tribalism and nationalism, are ancestor-consciousness gone septic or neurotic. It does no good for the comfortable and secure to try to eradicate this sort of consciousness, because in its healthy state it is a necessary part of human culture. It needs consecrating, not condemning. And the consecrating is achieved by Christ, who makes healing between himself and the people of the past; he makes healing between the people of the present and the images that they hold of the people of the past; and he makes healing between ancestral groups that have for generations been enemies. Every Eucharist is a celebration of this healing: it is the meeting place of the living and the dead, in the presence of the Lord who is the Lord of both. Translating all this into terms that can register with people who are attracted by, for instance, the National Front or the Provisional IRA is as tough an evangelistic task as any communicator has faced: but the basic truths and images are there.

At another point, Canon Wynne's experience accords closely to the apostolic model of preaching. The apostles preached in response to a question, a complaint, an initiative of some sort from the people whom they were with. Canon Wynne says quite baldly:

> Don't try to teach anyone until you have learned something from them. It's absolutely basic to get inside the other person's shoes, to try to see life through their eyes, to spend time in the situation of the person whom one longs to bring to Christ... That is why I have no confidence whatever in those nation-wide calls to evangelism, where everything is done on the top level and where people are thought of in the mass. If people are prepared to give other people their neighbourhood, then gradually by waiting on God, living close to them, they will see how they are going to proclaim the truths of Christianity to those people, and this will be different according to the particular community one is in.

You may think that this is an unnecessary statement of the obvious. I wish it were. But evangelistic enterprises continue to be spoiled at the outset by an impatient unwillingness to go through this stage, to go out empty, to listen. Evangelistic projects are designed with a timetable which allows for everything except this. And it is totally and absolutely essential. At the same time, those who make this sort of complaint about campaigns of evangelism sometimes seem to do so as an excuse for not getting into evangelism at all. Canon Wynne, at least, can't be accused of doing that. He lived and listened for seven years; and now there are communities of the baptized in ten out of the thirteen villages of those people.

This is a further point that we might note here. While it

is true that every church group ought to be concerned about evangelism and the spread of the Gospel, and in most cases ought to develop some sort of conscious policy about it, evangelism is never primarily a matter of special campaigns and organized planning. The tendency to see evangelism in military and commercial imagery is more likely to be part of the sickness than part of the remedy. We can talk about campaigns, deploying resources, cost-effectiveness, and so on. But the advance of the Gospel is almost always a surprise. Like the apostles, we find resistances where we thought we had allies, and we find people's hearts being opened where we had not included them in our plans.

When I have asked converts to tell how they came to Christian membership, more often than not the story has at its centre something which, from the angle of the ordinary standards of success, went wrong. There was courage and committedness, but nothing very impressive. 'The night I was "converted", I went along to a really awful, illogical, uninspiring evangelical talk. In spite of that, I was really made to change direction.' 'It was the sincerity and weakness, the mistakes and embarrassments, of two or three members of the Christian group that really impressed me.'

As Chesterton said — in words which remind us sharply of the absolute priority of the doctrine of justification by faith when we are involved in this sort of enterprise — 'If a thing is worth doing, it's worth doing badly'. We should, of course, desire and hope for the growth of our church, in the sense that we hope that people will indeed join us in recognizing Christ as Good News. But if we expect that this will happen through the perfection of our methods and the improvement of our resources, we are merely transferring into the church the methods and expectations of powerful and successful organisations of the world. This might be good news for the church: but the Gospel is good news for the poor, and the poor tend to be quick to size up people who merely want to organize them.

Primary evangelism still happens, and its disciplines are

far from being without significance for other areas. What is, however, more common is the stage where third- or fourth-generation Christians are criticizing the manner of Christianity which has been conveyed to them, and are seeking to discover more appropriate forms. This is not just anti-colonialism, it is not just syncretism; it is not just cultural games. The motive, in Africa and Asia, depends on a conviction that the Christ who has been proclaimed by the mission agencies is indeed Lord and Saviour: there is no going back on commitment to Christ. But the fullness of the meaning and the power of this Christ is not being disclosed yet; it is waiting for its more local embodiment.

At this point, there may well be points of contact with the Oxford Movement. That movement was shaped by a conviction that established religion in England had got an incorrect relationship between the two roles of church, the role of consecrator and the role of critic. It developed a more selective and self-conscious style of consecration, and it initiated a new vigour and precision of criticism. In this sense, the Oxford Movement shared features which are to be found in almost any movement of creative reform.

Beyond this, however, it would be unwise to press comparisons and analogies. One of the messages which comes through clearly from 'Third World' Christianity nowadays is that most of the traditional areas of argument and conflict between Western churches are irrelevant to their real needs. The sort of issues which traditionally have divided Catholics from Evangelicals in Britain often do not seem to be on the agenda within new situations. So it would be false pleading to point to any particular element in these contemporary explorations as a new triumph for the Catholic cause.

However, there is one other feature of these modern 'Third World' searchings which brings them into the same sort of atmosphere as that of the Oxford Movement. They are profoundly concerned with theology, not just with morality, ecclesiology, devotional life, and so on, but with the heartland of theology, the meaning of God and of God's revelation in Christ. And this is because theology must be an instrument of the just rule of God, the Kingdom declared in Jesus. The motive for the debate is not the need to get the terminology and the analogies right: the motive is to work towards the Kingdom in an environment which largely denies that Kingdom. The whole atmosphere is miles away from the gentlemanly exchange of opinions, which has often passed for the pursuit of truth in Western intellectual circles. Opinions do not fill bellies nor exorcise demons. They can provide material for discussion groups: but a discussion group which is not furthering the Kingdom is a cop-out from the real task of the church.

As an example, we could consider South African Black Theology. Catholics, both Anglican and Roman, have in fact made a considerable contribution to this movement. But so have Christians of other traditions; and Black Theology has been a criticism of standard Catholic theological teaching as much as of any other. In principle, it is a radical reclaiming of theology's traditional propositions, and therefore a renewing of our grasp upon them.

For instance, it is notorious that we Westerners find the doctrine of the Trinity very difficult to assimilate. On Trinity Sunday we make a nod to it; but for most of the time our image of God, in practice, is more like the solitary supreme being of Islam or of the Old Testament.

Why is this? Is it not that, in our culture, it is virtually impossible to conceive a power-structure that is not shaped like a pyramid? Our whole experience of power is that it requires a large number of units at the bottom, and only one at the top. The higher you go the fewer; the higher you go, the more subtle the differentials. There are far more privates than generals; but there are more ranks among generals than there are among privates. And the church, which represents God, is organized in the same way. Power works downwards; it becomes more diffused and more distant from its source, the lower it goes. We are told that God is Almighty: he is the super-general, the one who is above all generals and bishops: but, as God is the very apex of the power-pyramid, those who are fairly high up on the human pyramid will be closer to him than those who are in the lowest non-commissioned ranks. Generals and bishops have considerable rarity value, and may be a good deal more inaccessible than God!

We find it difficult not to see differences of rank even within the Trinity: it is difficult to conceive of a multiple model of power within which 'none is afore or after another: none is greater or less than another' (Athanasian Creed). Although we try to preach the Trinity, in the West we have more often been commending something more like Unitarianism, a God who is a solo point of power at the top of the system. Insofar as God has failed us, it is this kind of God who has failed.

But supposing there are people somewhere whose political experience is different, who live in a different kind of power-structure with different assumptions? Could this not rectify and renew our theology, and make the image of the Trinity more acceptable to our imagination? South African Black Theology may well be able to supply this, for the tribal system of black South Africa traditionally gives a lot of emphasis to the notion of power rising from below. That is not to say that there is no authoritarianism: there is, especially within the family. But, in the wider society of the tribe, there is a long, slow process by which the mind of the people is worked out and gathered together: the skill of the chief is not to lay down the rules and enforce them on the people, but to hear and to cohere the people, and to *be* the people in making pronouncements and in implementing the power which comes from below. The people are not just given a 'vote', i.e. an opportunity to make a choice between options which have been shaped by those who have power. Ordinary 'non-political' people participate in the political process a good deal more than most Westerners do — and, in spite of illiteracy and poverty, may therefore be more politically sophisticated than ordinary Europeans (the effects of this can be observed by anyone who has had to chair a church council of blacks and a church council of whites).

All this will not automatically rescue the Trinity from the doctrinal junkyard. But it can help us to grasp some fundamental themes again. The most important effect must surely be that an alternative image of power can show us that power can be corporate, that it does not have to be concentrated in a solo point of power. The heart of the doctrine of the Trinity is that supreme power is held in the manner of supreme love; and love cannot be love unless it is in some sense plural or corporate. To rehabilitate the doctrine of the Trinity, and to give it imaginative and persuasive power, we must have an image which makes it possible for the power-motive to fit into the love-motive and not (as is usually the case even in the best human structures) vice versa.

Further, this experience of power-from-below can deliver our doctrine of the incarnation from a tendency to describe Christ's incarnation as just a kind of foray or temporary visit. Belief in incarnation is not just belief in the divine presence in the world, important though that is: it is the wisdom of seeing that the divine programme works from the lowest levels upwards. In Christ, the power of God is found truly in the world, in the lowest and least significant, and rises to God bearing the pain and the complaint and the yearning of the human condition. Our intercession is included in Christ's intercession and extends it. In our intercession (this sounds a bit weird, but I think that this is merely because the imagery is unfamiliar) we participate in the political process of God; in other words, we involve ourselves in God's purposes, express our perception of the needs of God's community, and take our share in the working out of God's will, in God's power. Intercession, therefore, is a main element in the process of theosis, divinization, the taking of humanity into God. The claiming of this symbol-system can give proper place to several elements in traditional doctrine, such as the ascension of Christ and the intercession of the church, which do not fit conveniently into our conventional imagery of power.

I suggest also, that when African understandings of relationship are brought to bear on our trinitarian imagery, we shall feel more strongly that Western Christianity has been unwise to commit itself to the belief that the Spirit proceeds from the Father *and the Son*. One of the most important truths conveyed by the doctrine of the Trinity is that, although there is a source of being, the Father, this role of being source does not confer superiority of status. A world-view shaped by this insight would be a fundamental critique on most of our cultures; but a culture which gives more value to relatedness than to power has a better chance of seeing into this mystery.

Further, our conventional Western creed can be taken as implying that, as the Spirit proceeds from the Son as well as from the Father, the Spirit's operation is limited to situations where the Son is already known. This goes to the heart of one of the major sources of disagreement among missionaries. Many of us would want to deny this implication. But, if we believe that the Spirit is indeed to be recognized at work in situations where the Son is not yet known, we still insist that we are not just talking about any old spirit; we are talking about the Spirit who proceeds from the Father. And, in turn, we are not talking about any old 'father' — for father-images of God crop up in many cultures — we are talking of the one who is disclosed as Father by the Son. So I feel hesitant about confessing that the Spirit proceeds from the Father *and* the Son; but I see an excellent missionary motive in confessing that the Spirit proceeds from the Father *of* the Son. But, I do wish that the World Council of Churches, which has enabled some excellent dialogue on the *filioque*, would bring in its African resources at this point.[24] Here we could all gain new insight into old mysteries.

Black Theology is one realization of the hopes that were being expressed fifty years ago by people like the authors of *Essays Catholic and Missionary*, who were courageously looking forward to an era of invention, exploration, and learning, in the whole field of indigenization. Since then, there has been a good deal of practical experience, some of it within churches founded by missionaries, but more often within the Independent Churches. There has also been considerable development of 'African Theology' — a fairly academic kind of enterprise which operates in

European languages and affirms the continuities between Christianity and the networks of belief which guided Africa before Christianity came. Black Theology in South Africa shares some of these features: but, because it comes out of a situation of oppression it is a theology of hope and of change, not just a theology of affirmation. So it probably is safe from the most serious danger of 'indigenous' theologies, namely of undervaluing those elements in Christianity which are culturally new and discontinuous with the past — and these elements, of course, are mainly in the christological heartland of theology, which is as non-African and non-Asian as it is non-European.

Black Theology in South Africa must acknowledge its debt to the inspiration of the Black Theology of the United States. But its ability to claim an alternative model of power means that it can become more creative and radical than its American counterpart. The South African government has almost stifled Black Theology at birth, which shows its potential importance. But I think that it is worth consideration, as an example of the kind of renewal which can come to the heartland of traditional theology in a situation of mission and conflict in the overseas church.

We have considered two examples where traditional Catholic doctrine is illuminated by the experience of the church outside Europe. But there are other points at which the doctrinal emphases of Anglican Catholicism show signs of imbalance; they have been inadequate to meet the needs of overseas situations, and now need renewal to meet the needs of the Anglican situation in Britain.

The most urgent example of this concerns the doctrine of election.[25] British Anglicanism (which has to a large extent been English Anglicanism) has rather ignored this doctrine; it has not felt any great need for it, partly because it has, perhaps unconsciously, felt that the doctrine of election is irrelevant to the situation of a national church. Catholic Anglicanism, further, has been very suspicious of this element of doctrine, because it has been so vigorously claimed — and sometimes misused — within Protestantism.

But this doctrine is a key to understanding the role of the church within the world. And this is a matter on which the Church of England, despite a great deal of debate, has a confused mind.

Listen to any Church of England vicar talking about his work; he uses the word 'parish'. What does he mean? Sometimes he means the total population of the area — 'I have a parish of 11,000 people.' Sometimes he means the worshipping congregation at his own church — 'I hope that everyone in the parish will be praying for our new Bishop.' Sometimes he is thinking of a legally-defined area — 'You don't belong to this parish, so you can't get married here unless you are on the electoral roll.'

The word 'parish' has been exported; but, in the process, it has lost some of this range of meaning. To the question, 'How big is your parish?', the Church of England vicar will answer, '11,000'. To the same question, the priest outside England will answer, '300 families' — the number of people on the church roll. Outside England, we have clarified the meaning of the word 'parish'; we have domesticated it to be a purely ecclesiastical term. This means that we lose some of the Church of England's traditional sense of responsibility for all people, when we bend the word 'parish' away from its strict meaning of 'the total local population'. Probably, the Church of England will solve its confusion by sliding more and more into the non-English use of 'parish'; for the last generation or two it has been becoming more of a 'gathered church', and has been finding that its parish boundary-system is not particularly helpful to its mission in the urban areas. But this gain in clarity could mean a loss in commitment to mission, a loss of the responsibility expressed by the wider and more traditional meaning of the word 'parish'. At the same time, by paying lip-service to the traditional meaning of 'parish' while in practice working according to the narrower meaning, the Church of England may well be pretending to be more of a missionary church than it really is.

Effective mission depends, among other things, on having an intelligent understanding of the relationship between the congregation and the parish (in the traditional sense), that is, between the self-conscious church and the population in which it is set. Our confusion of language may hinder this.

While a church is some sort of established church or national church it will be kept to some extent outward-looking by the demands that come to it from outside its worshipping congregation. But if it becomes more of a 'gathered church', a congregational sect, it will need more deliberately vocational motives to remain a church-in-mission. Anglo-Catholicism has certainly become something like a 'gathered church' in some areas outside England; it has tended to follow a similar pattern in England as well.

Where a church is in danger of losing its sense of responsibility for the total population in which it is set, the remedy may well be that it should reaffirm its grasp of the doctrine of election, as part of Catholic doctrine.

The authentic New Testament theme of election has to be rescued from the tendancy within some presentations of Calvinism to see it primarily as a claim to privilege; according to this picture, the congregation of the faithful is chosen for blessedness, in contrast to the doom on the outsiders. When such a view is held by a church which is poor and oppressed, it can be part (although, even then, only a small part) of the realization of God's judgement and mercy. When such a view is held by a rich and powerful community set in the midst of a poorer majority, it is so ugly that one begins to feel that the doctrine of election is too dangerous and that it ought to be thrown away.

Further, the doctrine of election has been picked up by people who, for one reason or another, are attracted by the notion of a world governed by immutable laws. God's choice, made at the beginning of time, shapes a deterministic universe, our dreams of freedom are fantasies, and our claims to be able to make choices are false. This depends on a picture of God whose creativity was totally spent in the original creating, and who is no longer the creator. This picture claims divine sanction for an unchanging order, and it is attractive to those for whom the system works. Those for whom the system does not work have to overthrow such a picture, at least in their own minds, before they can work for change.

Such a world-view of determinism and fatalism receives powerful support from schools of psychology and sociology which aim at maximizing their ability to predict and generalize. They do not necessarily insist that you are nothing but the product of predictable forces and mechanisms; but they do give people the sense that all that is worth knowing about themselves is that which can be identified in this manner. Casting off the shackles of one determinism, they become trapped by another. Those who do the investigating have power over those who are investigated; and the process works in terms which the powerful set up. The effect is similar to that of the deterministic exposition of the doctrine of election, where all the announcements and classifications are made by those for whom the system is advantageous.

When a doctrine gets distorted like this, it is not because the basic doctrine is false in itself. The problem is that its exponents have detached it from Christ, from the mission and the purpose and the style of Christ, and have let it follow an autonomous logic. The authentic New Testament doctrine is based firmly in the figure of Christ. The main theme of the doctrine (e.g. in Ephesians 1) is not that some have been chosen and others totally rejected, but that one has been chosen and others are chosen in him. Through him and in him, groups of Christians have been chosen, to share in his mission, his rejection, his suffering, and his hope. The church is chosen as Christ is chosen, for the same purposes. Therefore the church and its members should never feel that their chosenness is primarily for their own advantage: it is so that the activity of God in Christ may continue.

The reason for this lies deep in the Christian doctrine of God and the Christian understanding of humanity. The most important of all truths about God, more important than God's power, omniscience or glory, is that God is relatedness. God is love. God is Trinity. Creation, redemption and the coming of the Kingdom are the extending of this relationship. Human beings are designed for relationship. Blessedness — and this is a point where Christianity differs very sharply from many religious systems of the world, especially in the East — does not consist in being removed from the world of relationships into a purer realm of solitary glory or absorption into the divine. Blessedness is in relationship itself. And communication from God to a person is normally through another person, not by some sort of direct ray. This is why the knowledge of God is so closely tied up with community life. It is in the healthiness of the community life that the knowledge of God is registered. It is not an intellectual or spiritual possession which one can improve on one's own.

This is the main value of that precious item in the Catholic's tool-box, the apostolic succession. Unfortunately it has suffered from being used by one group of Christians to knock another group on the head with. Any doctrine which is used and valued primarily as a means of scoring points in arguments among Christians is bound to be damaged and devalued. At its truest, the doctrine of the apostolic succession is the humble incarnational witness that the truth of God is passed from person to person, neighbour to neighbour, and there is never a radical total new start. The apostolic succession institutionalizes this truth: and if we believe in incarnation, we have to accept that truths need to be institutionalized: they do not just remain ideas in the head. The problem in overseas mission has been that apostolic succession has meant European succession: in many areas, this has eventually worked out all right. But, in the Belgian Congo, for instance, the Christ whom the missionaries proclaimed could not be seen as one of *us*, an African, until there was a break at least at the institutional level. So there came into being the Kimbanguist Church, in the earlier years of this century. After a lengthy phase of being outside the Catholic or ecumenical fellowship, they now value their membership of the World Council of Churches, along with European-based churches. At the level of apostolic authority, the succession broke, as with so many independent churches; but healing proves to be possible, once people come to feel that Christ truly is of their culture and speaks with their accent.

The doctrine of election means that salvation works through community, through person-to-person contact, starting with Jesus. And this is a scandal to those who want to see God giving each individual an equal chance. Individuals do not all get an equal chance: some are within range of the communicating team and some are not. But the method of the message would not be true to its content if the message could be mechanically smeared all over the world at once without any real basis in human relatedness. That, in passing, is the fatal disadvantage of those forms of evangelism which substitute technology for personal contact. 'I have been preaching to African mineworkers from loudspeaker vans for over twenty years,' an evangelist said to me once, 'and I still cannot tell one black face from another.' And it's not just the newer technologies that present the danger: books and religious buildings can have the same effect.

Salvation is people being opened to each other. This theme runs through the gospels, in the events of success and of failure in Jesus' ministry. And those who are already *in* depend for their salvation on the arrival of those who are not in. In the pattern of mission the Jew is chosen first and then the Gentile. But the Jew then had to be willing almost to start all over again, in a community in which the Gentile is there first. Romans 9—11 cannot just be written off as a bit of ruminating about a painful problem of centuries ago. Every group that is now an inheritor of an old Christian tradition of discipleship has to work out how it relates to the new groups coming in: and it may have to realize that its true hope is in the old becoming attached to the new, not in the new being attached to the old. Those who are the elect have their hope of salvation in their relationship with those who are not (or not yet) the elect.

In our proclamation in these days, there is one form of human hope and yearning to which we must address ourselves with all the clarity and compassion that we can muster. It is a hope and yearning which inspires millions of people and which motivates much of their ambitions and choices. I mean, the hope that one can achieve blessedness by separating oneself from the common lot of humankind. Ethnic and national classifications are valued because of their power to give superior status. This is one of the main inspirations behind racism: it can put appalling burdens on persons whose racial classification is in doubt. Educational and financial achievements offer a similar kind of rescue. Moral and religious dedication can be most attractive of all as a way to detach oneself from the majority, especially perhaps for those who have no other options. I can't belong to the right race, nation or class; I can't get education or wealth: but I can be good; I can be faithful to my religion. This accounts, I believe, for the surprisingly deep interest among British Christian students in such questions as, Who gets to heaven and who goes to Hell, and how do you tell the difference? And we should have some sympathy with them. There is a doom over the human race, and in every age there have been people who seek to make some sort of nuclear fall-out shelter for themselves.

The Gospel recognizes this doom: 'In Adam all die'. But the answer is not that safety is for the elect or for refugees from the human race: the answer is, 'In Christ will all be made alive' (1 Corinthians 15:21). And the second 'all' must mean, in the hope and purpose of the Gospel, the same range of persons as the first 'all'. There is, therefore, a promise of salvation: but it is not for those who wish to have salvation in separateness from the rest of the human race. The hope is in Christ, the Second Adam, who is the representative of all the human race. We get salvation, not by the fortuitous fact that we happen to be within range of the apostolic team, but because Christ is our representative, representing every human being.

And the same principle continues in the elect, the Body of Christ. They are set in the middle of a lump of the world's population representing it, present within it as Jesus was present in the world, feeling and suffering and hoping with the rest of the population, present there as a means whereby the meaning of God's purpose can be made known within the wider population. They cannot be the church without deep personal contact with those whom they represent. Their salvation is bound up with the salvation of those around them. They are being saved as part of the process whereby those around them are being saved as well. They will not feel total failures just because they are small in number: but they will not allow their smallness to make them feel self-sufficient and unrelated to the tragic world around. They will pray for it: they will bring the world around into their more conscious life in God: and they will seek opportunity to disclose this in a way which, hopefully, will make sense to those among whom they are placed. They will proclaim the truth as they see it, not primarily in order to increase the size of their organization but because they see that people are being left hungry, and sometimes are being really destroyed, by false myths and corrupting forms of hope. Thus they will turn the confusion between 'congregation' and 'parish' to advantage: a sound doctrine of election encourages us to recognize the difference of function but also warns us against relying on a difference of identity or of status. The blurred edge should keep us human, content with the humanity of Christ.

12   The Mission and the Medium: Words

The manner of the communication says as much as the content. The Catholic movement did not have to wait for Marshall McLuhan to tell us this. Incarnation means that truth is fully to be known only in flesh, in action. It is no good getting the content right if it is being denied by the style or the process.

Incarnation did not stop with the Ascension. Pentecost saw the enfleshment of the Word in the new community. It was a community essentially marked by its variety. The forming of a new community out of many languages is one of the continuing signs of the Spirit's work. In our day, it happens most obviously when people move around and form new groups away from home. This is sometimes due to a terror that they leave behind, as in the case of the Hambukushu exodus-community. Sometimes it is due to the compulsion of political forces or the attraction of economic advantage. These influences have considerably affected church work overseas in the last fifty years or so. For instance, I mentioned earlier the congregation of migrant mineworkers that I once served. They came from all over Southern and Central Africa. There were never less than six languages represented in our worship. Normally the sermon was offered through interpreters in four languages, and hymns sung in six. And everybody took this pattern for granted.

The church itself has felt a divine calling to come together in larger associations: overseas dioceses which previously related individually to Canterbury have come together to make Provinces. This has not been without difficulty and set-back — but also not without miracle; Bishop Leslie

Stradling, a former Bishop of Johannesburg who was previously Bishop of South-West Tanganyika, tells of this process:

> Men had for years discussed the formation of a Church Province in East Africa, but negotiation had always broken down long before they came to a point of decision. The geographical and ecclesiastical difficulties were too great for men to overcome them. When in 1960 the Province suddenly — as men count it — came into being, it seemed to us that just such another miracle as Pentecost had taken place. God had spoken to us and we all had heard his voice in our own tongue — Kikuyu, Gogo, English, Bondei, Makua, Nyasa — and we were amazed at the mighty works of God.[26]

The development of Anglican Provinces has been more than just a growth in administrative efficiency and economy — sometimes it seems to have had rather opposite effects! Nor has it been merely a matter of following secular processes, of decolonization and independence. The really important growth has been in catholicity, in the widening of the range of people who live and work together within a single inclusive structure. Variety of language, of imagery, and culture become positive blessings instead of luxuries or inconveniences.

This itself says something about Christ and the Gospel. In Christ, God has put his own meaning into a context where continuously it has to be translated. And translation is not just a matter of taking a lump of meaning out of one pot and putting it, unchanged, into another. The Welsh word for 'translator' — *cyfieithwr* — really suggests the sharing of language, the putting of two languages together, alongside each other. Translation is the 'being-together' of two languages, so that one illuminates and renews the message of the other. There is, for instance, no single clear doctrine of Christ, or of salvation, or of the Holy Spirit, in the New Testament. There is a whole range of images and models and languages which are laid alongside each other, and are translations of each other. Even in the New Testament, there are plenty of signs that the meaning of Christ could never be totally summed up in the culture and language of the Hebrew-thinking people of first-century Judaea. Translation recognizes that there are things to be gained by the language from which translation is made as well as by the language into which translation is made.

The whole debate summed up in Acts 15, for instance, is about whether 'uncircumcision' or 'paganism' has some identity and value in itself, or whether it has to assimilate to Judaism in order to acquire value. The decision is made quite clearly, that paganism does not have to forget its own identity and adopt Jewish identity. Both accept a new identity in Christ, who calls them to be alongside each other in one catholicism. The Jews give up their insistence on Gentiles accepting Jewish identity; Gentiles give up specific practices which would make fellowship with them impossible for Jews.

The sensitivities here are in several ways similar to those of the system, noted earlier, which was worked out by Bishop Lucas of Masasi; in allowing East African Christians to retain their dances and initiation schools and so on, he was not making a concession or a soft option, nor was he being just paternalistically indulgent towards an 'inferior' race. He was basically concerned to make a clear difference 'between winning souls to Christ and denationalizing them'. And he therefore saw the need to work out the New Testament pattern in this new context, holding to Paul's belief in the positive contribution to be made by the new culture into which the Gospel is taken.

By its handling of the 'Gentile problem' of its own day, the New Testament church demonstrated, for all successive generations, that the good news in Christ is designed and intended to reach and to be meaningful within every culture and language group of the human race. There is no single holy language. No one has to abandon his or her home-language in order to speak the holy truth — though, on occasion, for the sake of catholic community, we may well rejoice to be led in prayer and worship in a language other than our home-language, and even in a language which we do not understand at all.

Anglican Catholicism has treasured this understanding of catholicism. It has used English as a *lingua franca*; but it has never wanted to see English as a new kind of Latin. It has put a lot of urgency into translation, not of the Bible so much as of the liturgy, with the necessary scripture readings. Worship, not education, has been the first priority.

In Britain, one of the most serious accusations which can be levelled against Anglo-Catholicism is that it has tended to encourage dependency, to make people feel that they cannot practise their religion or say prayers unless they are making maximum use of the provisions of a sacerdotal technology. Christian education has at times been a programme for making people dependent on that which only a professional priest with an authorized formulary can provide.

The same problem has certainly had its effect overseas. In some ways it has been worse there: we have taught people the central importance of the Mass, and then have provided it for them only quarterly. But in other ways the dependence has been less serious. Partly, this is because the very shortage of priests means that people cannot expect the maintenance of the 'standards' of the Anglo-Catholicism of south-east England. In practice, people's day-to-day spirituality is, in rural areas at least, not shaped by a specialist priest but by the local catechist, who is very much part of the local community, sharing their background and education. And partly there is less dependency on the priest overseas because there is not the same degree of interdenominational rivalry (due, in the big British cities, to people's powerful need for a clear identity over against the mass of the population) which makes some British Catholics so scared of doing anything which might look nonconformist. And partly it is because the poor have more confidence in their own voice and their own language; although there are hierarchies and status systems, and although language differences are certainly used, as shibboleths, to detect friend and foe, there is nothing quite like the English class system which has made so many people feel that their language or accent is something to be ashamed of. And it is partly because Christians of young churches know that even an authoritarian form of Christianity has come as a form of deliverance and therefore it must have some sort of freedom in it.

However it may be, confidence in one's own language and freedom in approach to God are among the blessings brought by our missions, either because of or in spite of their styles of worship. This is beautifully illustrated by another Pentecost-style story of Bishop Stradling:

> There was an old Tanzanian woman who was too infirm to go to church. A priest who was bringing her the sacrament approached soundlessly along the sandy track that led to her hut, and he paused outside as he heard a voice within and thought that there was a visitor. But it was the old woman praying aloud, and this is what he heard her say: 'Dear Lord, I don't know whether you can understand Makua, but that is the only language which I know, so I must talk to you in that. And I want to tell you in Makua that I love you like my last-born child.'[27]

That, I suggest, is the sign of a Christian who has totally taken on board the message of Pentecost, the message of God's acceptance of our own most personal language. And no professional experts are going to disable her!

This receptive attitude to culture and language does not mean that we suspend our ability to assess, discriminate and judge. There is a kind of 'liberal' who will try to see good in everything; this would deprive us of our duty to criticize racism or the exploitation of children. Those who attack Christianity for passing judgement on people's natural cultures must be asked whether they extend this same generosity towards the present culture of the Afrikaners. No. Christ is the fulfilment of the creative yearnings of every culture. But Christ is also a misfit within every culture. The problem in our mission is that he has appeared to be more European than African, more middle-class than working-class, more male than female, just as he appeared in the early days of the church to be more Jewish than Gentile. But he actually was the most complete misfit among Jewish society, because it was that society which pushed him out and crucified him. The message to, for instance, Galatian Gentiles, was that Christ would be a misfit for them also if they sought to take to themselves the lifestyle and the exclusiveness of the Jews. Christ comes as critic as well as fulfiller.

Paul's own pilgrimage is typical of the experiences of many missionaries. He started life as a Jew. He became a Gentile in order to communicate with Gentiles: and he also *became* a Jew in order to communicate with Jews (I Corinthians 9:20). He had to repossess his own cultural possession. And the main reason for this was his encounter with an outside culture. Similarly, someone has noted that Bataks on becoming Christians, not only remain Batak but *become* Batak.[28] But this self-consciousness is not a pretext for an uncritical nationalism. On the contrary, when Paul *becomes* a Jew he is then free to scrutinize and evaluate Judaism from within, to see its deep sickness and the available remedies. Missionaries, like Paul, will identify Christ as the critic who is most severe on his own culture when that culture makes other people's culture abnormal or second-rate.

As the Oxford Fathers saw, Christ is most characteristically critic within a culture when that culture takes its dominance for granted. They insisted that Christ would be critical of the growing secularity of their time. There is no reason to suppose that Christ would be any less of a misfit in the value-free scientific culture which the West has cherished in more recent years. Intellectually this culture may be immensely impressive: it has developed structured justice on a wide scale. But it has also resulted in great damage to the planet; and it has produced weapons which threaten the human race as never before.

So, while Christ is indeed critic of all our languages and cultures, his bias is to be critic of those who have the power to offer him as a specimen or archetype of their normal, powerful culture. Christ's story shows that they are likely to be the crucifiers.

13   The Mission and the Medium: Institutions

Perhaps the greatest difference between the New Testament church and the present-day church is that the latter has become an employer and a landowner. Whether we like it or not, this is part of the church's statement about itself. Rightly, we reflect carefully on what different styles of church building are perceived as saying. But there is a prior message which is conveyed by a church building of any size and style, namely that someone somehow has secured rights over this bit of land and has had the wealth to erect a building on it. Even in Britain, church buildings have an economic message; in some instances, such as the 'stint churches' in Lancashire, the message is consciously interpreted, to the effect that this house of God was built out of the profits made on working people's poor wages. In areas where land is held publicly by a tribe, the meaning of a church building can be still more undesirable; possession of land by colonizers had frequently been the result of either military or economic conquest. The church's land-tenure has sometimes been part of this process. British people tend to be sophisticated and shrewd about questions of wages and salaries, and strangely naive about land-tenure. When they go overseas as missionaries, they have to learn something of the realistic and sensitive way in which people in many other parts of the world recognize issues of land-tenure; often, it is the surest guide to the whole way in which a population is organized. And basically, of course, the same is true in Britain. Any church-in-mission, in Britain or overseas, needs to ask carefully how its physical presence is seen and understood, especially by those who are outside its fellowship. This is particularly true if, as is the case in some cities in India, the church is a small minority of the population and yet holds considerable pieces of land.

The Catholic movement, in its overseas outreach, has normally contented itself with building quite modest church-buildings. Occasionally it has been more ambitious, and has put up a more elaborate kind of 'shrine-church' — a building very different to other buildings around, a building which is intended to speak of the beauty of holiness. Such a building offers for consecration all sorts of skills; it says things about the divine presence incarnate which words cannot say. And this is very precious and valuable. The problem is that Anglican Catholicism has been very closely identified with one particular theory and movement in nineteenth-century architecture in England, a movement which propagated the conviction that there was only one style appropriate for Christian worship. The Protestant tradition has, perhaps, felt rather more free to let the building speak in local languages. But, logically, Catholicism's instinct for consecrating the natural order should have led it to be more culturally adaptable than in practice it usually has been.

Six hundred years ago, the Gothic system was the most efficient available for covering in a large building; but it is now an exceptionally expensive method: even a very simple Gothic-style building can present almost impossible problems when it is the only building of its type for hundreds of miles, when there is no one locally who has experience of handling materials in this style, and when it reaches an age when major faults develop. All the decisions about the location, the style, the building and the financing of the structure were made perhaps sixty years ago by people who had no roots in the area. And now the present church population has both to maintain the building and cope with the fact that, in style and manner, it may well be saying something quite different to what they want to say.

Major church buildings usually are found alongside church administration systems; and these also have a message. They can give the sense that the church has arrived in the commercial world, that it operates in the style of competitive business, and that those who do not belong in that world are likely to be second-class citizens in the church also. At our college in Selly Oak, we have had students from the 'Third World' who have been surprised and rather delighted to find us operating an office with much more primitive equipment than they were used to in their new administrative outfits back home. When I was a college principal, the weakness that I was most conscious of in myself was sheer incompetence in management skills. I do not despise such skills at all: I believe that administration is a gift of the Spirit, and that bad management is a poor witness to the Spirit. But a church-in-mission must beware of the kind of administration which makes poor people feel that they are being managed — for this is the feeling that they get from other structures virtually every hour of their lives. Few things are more likely to deny the content of the message which we seek to proclaim.

Any church property raises this sort of problem. Just over fifty years ago, Bishop Philip Loyd of Nasik was offering a precise warning to those agencies, with money to spare, who planned to set up medical or educational work in India: 'They must not embark upon, and they must be content not to have, institutions of such magnitude and elaborate efficiency as will for ever be beyond the power of the Indian Church to maintain. There is a real call for self-denial on the part of the doctor or educationist just out from England. The money is available; the way is clear; the manpower is available. But pause and think. Are you twisting a leading-string or forging a fetter? These fine new white buildings, whom do you mean to be responsible for their overhaul and repair fifty years hence?'[29] Bishop Loyd's fifty years hence has arrived now. Let us, in this day, have the same solicitude for our Christian descendants of 2030 AD!

One of the best reasons for having a church building is that it is a place where the church has the freedom to express itself in whatever language it needs, without having to get anyone else's permission. This is particularly important in connection with visual language. Within the church building, works of art are protected from the myth which is generated by museums and art galleries, that works of art can and should have an independent life, detached from the purposes that brought them into being. A church-in-mission uses the language of painting and sculpture to say things which must be said but which words cannot say, particularly on the theme that Christ is one of *us* and that his kingdom has a claim on the real world which we know and inhabit. For instance, the west window of St Michael's, Tividale, shows the Virgin Mary against a background of factory chimneys and smoke, with the words 'Queen of the Black Country, pray for us' — a remarkable statement from the late Victorian era.

A similar statement of the localness of the Gospel has been generated by Cyrene School in Zimbabwe, which gave great freedom and encouragement to black people to portray the Gospel story with black persons and in black terms. This is not merely an evangelistic device to communicate better with illiterate natives — although this is not to be despised. The deeper meaning is that, in visual terms as well as verbal terms, the honour and the god-likeness of these people is affirmed: they are, as much as anyone else, made in the image of God. And when most other signals have been insisting on their inferiority, this artistic message must have powerful overtones for social change.[30]

Similarly with the communication through music. Catholicism has long insisted that the truth of a song cannot be known except in singing it; it has encouraged singing not just on the fringes but at the heart of liturgy. English people are divided in their judgement about this. Singing is good: but it is also a field of professional expertize, and there are many who feel silenced rather than enabled by the choir's performance. This says more about the English habit of professionalizing and institutionalizing than it says about singing in itself. I was told by a wise catechist when I first went to celebrate the Eucharist in one of our South African out-stations: 'If you get the congregation to sing the Mass, you will cut out those who can't sing: if you get them to say it, you will cut out those who can't read.'

This is important not only when many are illiterate but also when people of several languages are forming one congregation. All over Central and Southern Africa, in twenty or more languages, congregations large and small still express the core of the faith through the simple and adaptable Mass-setting first invented by Fr Woolley, SSJE. For migratory workers, this is far more important than any official uniformity in the words of the prayers. This is one point where the effect of Catholicism in music has been totally opposite to a disabling by experts. Sadly, the one group which has shut itself off from this music is the whites. White students from that part of Africa sing it for the first time when they come to Birmingham! Perhaps whites feel that they do not need to use such a setting because they are secure in the universality of English.

However, the universal can be the enemy of the local. It can discourage variety and inventiveness. It can inhibit the use of the language of our place and of our time. Localness of time is as important as localness of place, and it was this that inspired the Twentieth Century Church Light Music Group thirty years ago. This also was an initiative with a Catholic instinct. Some of its hymn-tunes are turning out to be its most durable product: but, in terms of its main purpose, its most important work was its Mass-settings. The fact that those went out of date fairly quickly is no condemnation; what the group was doing was, properly, ephemeral. Significant origins are usually fragile and quickly buried. There was an essentially missionary motive in this enterprise, which encouraged similar attempts at indigenization outside Britain. Indeed both Gerard Beaumont and Patrick Appleford were able to offer their distinctive contribution in mission service overseas, in Stellenbosch and Lusaka.

With its great wealth of indigenous music from the past, English Christian culture is not able to move very fast, particularly in the field of Mass-settings. For both Latin and English Catholicism, the movement into indigenous language in Europe and Britain has caused something of an aesthetic desert. In Africa, particularly in the Roman Communion, it has been a priceless blessing. Fr Adrian Hastings, whose knowledge of Christianity in Africa is uniquely wide, and who is not given to uncritical enthusiasm, claims that the way in which the Roman Catholic church has transformed its church music is 'perhaps the single most encouraging thing that has happened in African Christianity' during the 1970s. And he makes it clear that his standard of judgement is not aesthetic but is the essential communication of the Gospel.[31]

14 The Mission and the Medium: Education

Most Christian missions in Africa and Asia have mission stations or mission compounds. The typical mission station has three main units — the church, the hospital, and the school. The school is, of course, part of the total instrument of proclamation; part of its aim has always been to provide a place of evangelistic activity towards the younger generation. But it has also been founded, like the hospital, on the understanding that education, like healing, is a gift of God to be dispensed through the church.

This is not the place to enter a thorough evaluation of the mission schools. It is extremely easy, with hindsight, to be critical of them. Governments have had very mixed feelings about them: they have envied them, and so have taken them over; they have distrusted and suspected them of encouraging political criticism, and so have taken them over; they have been worried about their poverty and incompetence, and so have taken them over; they have suspected them of representing an alien culture, and sometimes a culture of social class-consciousness, and so have taken them over. For one reason or another, missions now have far fewer schools to look after than they had fifty years ago. But the most serious criticism is one which affects the whole character of our educational assumptions when judged according to the norms of a healthy community; and this, therefore, is a judgement which has to be heard in the context of our proclamation of the Gospel.

Let us take the judgement of President Nyerere of Tanzania on the kind of education which was brought into his country by colonial and mission agencies. Firstly, it induced attitudes of inequality, and encouraged the domination of the weak by the strong, particularly in the economic field; it did not encourage the development of a single nation; and it took participants in education away from the heart of Tanzanian society. Secondly, the education system made students ignorant or scornful of the traditional wisdom of the ordinary farmer. 'The pupil absorbs beliefs about witchcraft before he goes to school, but he does not learn the properties of local grasses; he absorbs the taboos from his family but does not learn the methods of making nutritious traditional foods. And from school he acquires knowledge unrelated to agricultural life. He gets the worst of both systems!'[32]

President Nyerere's critique is of great interest as a piece of mission-in-reverse; it applies just as seriously to the education systems of the European countries which exported their educational methods and assumptions to Africa.

What is of particular interest in the context of our present study is that many of the President's criticisms were anticipated forty years earlier by Bishop Frank Weston of Zanzibar, who claimed that 'education as preached at present will be Africa's curse.'[33] The main reason for this was that people are designed for and born into a system of relationships: traditional education nurtured people within these relationships, but imported styles of education were extracting people from them. So an integrated society was being replaced by a society dominated by experts who had no real bonds with tribe, nation or land.

The church has, on the whole, much less formal work in ordinary schooling than it had fifty years ago. What remains is still subject to Nyerere's and Weston's criticism. One of the sad things about the church's contribution to education is that often it starts as a service to the poor and becomes a service to the privileged. This pattern is so common, both in Britain and overseas, that the church has to reckon it as an occupational hazard which will probably threaten any educational exercise which it cares to set up. It has constantly to watch the effect of its educational presence. There are still places overseas to which missionary teachers from Britain can go. But, particularly in Asia, it seems that these are to a large extent residential institutions, big expensive Christian foundations. It must be very difficult for such places to avoid giving the impression that the sort of educational enterprise which British Christians are most interested in supporting is the sort of education which serves those who are already well off.

This message is, fortunately, counterbalanced by the way in which all sorts of other forms of education have developed in recent years. The church now has, probably, as many workers involved in these other forms of education as it ever had in its schools.

Adult education, leadership training, literacy work, and other forms of 'alternative education' flourish in many parts of the church, and represent a new reponse to this old element in our calling. In particular, the church has in several areas pioneered the kind of leadership training which helps people to recognize and practise the skills of co-operation rather than competition. This is a necessary antidote to the sort of experience which Nyerere and Weston complain of. It also enables, indeed it encourages, people to question given structures and to claim their ability to make their own contribution. By nourishing this sort of education, the church establishment has stimulated a good deal of internal self-criticism; the whole trend of it runs contrary to the assumptions of fixed authority. But this is needed not only for the good of the church; by enabling such education, the church is helping to provide a supply of people who are alert and critical about the operation of authority in society as a whole.

And we in Britain need the benefit of the kind of criticism developed by people like Nyerere. While we had full employment, the problem was obscured. But now the biggest divide among young people is between those who have had the luck to get jobs and those who haven't, and we can see, very close to home, the dangers of an educational system which is geared to producing experts and competitors. The industrial system no longer absorbs them; their qualifications are like the powerful engines inside the surplus vehicles which stand unsold outside our car assembly plants. And our educational system doesn't give people the skill to live within that sort of situation. In education, the church has often been a pioneer, doing things that other agencies have not had the vision or the means to do. Can it become a pioneer in Britain again, benefiting from its contacts with education in the poor world, leading the way in preparing people for the exercise of the skills not of competition, prestige, and expert status, but of co-operation and the formation of community? And this is our next theme.

THE FORMING OF COMMUNITY

15   The Vision of Community

Community-formation is no extra to the Gospel. It is the aim and the product of all the church's work.

Community is the test of mission. And it is not a vague niceness for those who like to be friendly. The essential character of community, and therefore of love, in the New Testament, is that it brings people together and holds people together who would otherwise have little in common. It is the overcoming of separation. It is the continuing of Christ's own programme.

Community is controversial: it means attacking those powers which prefer separation and which inhibit real meeting. Community is creative: it pushes back the boundaries of chaos and of isolation.

Community restores the balance of the church's life. In its proclaiming and its healing work, the church is performing tasks; inevitably, it tends to give value to those people who can best enable it form these tasks. In the mission hospital, the doctor is bound to have a certain status and authority by virtue of her medical role. But in its community-function, the church will insist that the doctor is no more important than anyone else. This is a rather harsh example: on a mission station, it is not unknown for a doctor not be allowed to be anything but doctor. If the doctor is an unmarried woman, she may find it very difficult indeed to insist upon being anything other than her role. But she must do, or else there is a danger that everyone else who can claim a role will do so all the time: and those who have no identifiable role will be second-class citizens — a constant problem for the old, the stupid, the misfit.

The church, in its community-function, will refuse to

judge people by their usefulness; in fact, it may well upset the ordinary roles. The church tends to say that if a person is dealing with money in the secular world, that person should be expected to handle the church's money. If the church is looking for someone to teach in a children's class, it will call on those who teach in ordinary school. Consequently, when it wants someone for pouring out tea, it will select someone who already does little else except pour out tea. So the church merely emphasises all the roles, stereotypes and imbalances in society, and does nothing to widen people's range of skills. Church-as-community will widen the community of potential skills within each person: it will give a voice to the scholar who is silently trapped inside the peasant, and give an opportunity to come into the open to the peasant who is locked up inside the scholar. This, in itself, is mission. It is disclosing some of the hidden potential in the created order.

In passing, one of the most satisfying things about being a white missionary in the 'Third World' is that you never know what you may have to turn your hand to next. Any ability you may possibly have is likely to be claimed, and you learn all sorts of skills which you never dreamed of before. Conversely, it is often depressing for the returning missionary to come back into a culture where there are experts to do everything, a culture which has become institution-dependent rather than neighbour-dependent.

An apparently 'simple' culture is often skilful at enabling people to have roles and thus to have value. African children, for instance, take responsiblity for younger brothers and sisters from quite a tender age, much as used to be the custom in working-class Britain. Expatriate missionaries may well be embarrassed to discover that their own children get more food and more schooling than African children of the same age, but that they are less responsible and less able to look after themselves or after anyone else. When the more 'democratic' Western churches become really indigenized overseas, they sometimes become more hierarchical. Methodism in West Africa, for instance, has developed not only bishops and archbishops but a patriarch.

This does not necessarily mean a loss of community and an increase in authoritarianism. It can mean the development of a complex system of roles in which individuals have more sense of a place and a responsibility than they would have in a featureless bureaucracy. This is the value — at least for males — of the variety of roles provided in the traditional High Mass, and the churches of Africa and Asia may be right in their instinct to be conservative at this point. And part of the point of these liturgical roles is that they do not depend much on skill or educational status. A professor can be the acolyte, and (and this is a quite genuine example which one can find in independent churches in Britain as well as overseas) a railwayman on night-shift may be the bishop.

In mission, it is important to hold to the fact that we belong in our community by the grace and mercy and love of God, and not by our deserving. Our doctrine of baptism proclaims this. We sometimes hear an objection to Christian faith in terms such as these: Why must you be so exclusive? Surely the good Hindu deserves as much favour and recognition as any Christian? And the crude answer has to be, Why bring goodness into it? You are proposing that if a Hindu is good enough he should be put onto the same level as a Christian. But a Christian doesn't get his or her place in the community by virtue of goodness. The grace of God is always a surprise. In the New Testament, the conscientious followers of the law are the people who have most problems: it is the sinners who recognize something special in Christ and who find their way into his community. This is not just a matter of a rather perverse theory. It is obvious in missionary practice, that we run into confusion and disappointment if we try to judge which individuals are saved and which are not, particularly if we try to do so in terms of good behaviour or sincerity. The Gospel witness is that the bad Hindu can be saved neither less nor more than the good one, and that, if the Christians put themselves as a distinct religious sect over against the Hindus, we have to go on to say that the Hindus can be saved neither less nor more than the Christians. The Christian community is primarily a community which knows and witnesses to the purpose and method of God's salvation. It is not a body which exists to define its boundaries and to make announcements about the fate of those who are outside them.

Catholicism puts an essential stress on universality and availability for all: it is fundamentally different to national or racial or even religious definition. It says that God meets people (and that therefore the church must meet people) in terms of what we have in common, our createdness, our alienation, our sharing in the sin and frustration of the world, not in terms of our religious specialness or success. There are, of course, massive differences in our religious systems. But when people meet in virtue of their religions as such, the chances are that they have an interesting discussion which gives special opportunity for those with expert knowledge to display it. They do not necessarily meet deeply as persons, and they do not necessarily achieve any unity except a unity of those who are good at discussion, over against those who are not personally cast in that mould. In colleges and universities in Britain, I have known Christian students agonize for hours about the question of whether they could join in prayers with Muslims. For a priest from Malaŵi there was no problem, because he was used to occasions in Malaŵi when Christians and Muslims would share in public prayer, meeting each other not primarily as Christians or Muslims but as fellow-members of a village. To seek a unity of religions as such could well be a diversion from the real need for a unity of human beings based on a struggle against injustice and poverty. And religiousness — including Christian religiousness, Anglican religiousness, and very definitely Anglo-Catholic religiousness — often displays more the alienation from which we need to be delivered than the new humanity into which Christ is leading us.

One of the biggest problems with the whole notion of community is that it inevitably raises questions of membership and identity. Baptism is a mark of membership. It says who is in, and therefore also says something about who is out. Where the community of the baptized (or of those who affirm their baptism) is very small, members usually share a strong sense of membership. Where the number of the baptized is large and diffused, and there is not much sense of specific Christian community, the 'church' is likely to be seen as a small group of specialist professionals serving humanity in general.

There are dangers with every type of community design. Features of Christian discipleship which are entirely good in themselves can be co-opted into our insistent need to know who is *in* and who is *out*. The offer of 'full Catholic privileges' can be received as a way of rewarding me for being what I am and for not being what I am not. Anglo-Catholicism has at times appealed to the same sort of desire which led the Galatian Christians to seek and value circumcision — a desire to have a clear insignia to tell us who is *in* and who is *out*.[34]

In our Mission Training programme at Selly Oak, I have for five years conducted a course on the Letter to the Galatians; each time, I have asked students to face this question, among others: 'What, in your experience of the church today, corresponds to circumcision as it was experienced in the Galatian church?' What feature is used as a means of sharpening up our identity and of showing who are the 'real' Christians and who aren't? There were always some students who answered in terms of moral attitudes or denominational allegiances. But I have to say, with surprise and sadness, by far the most common answer was, the pressure to behave in a 'charismatic' manner. And this answer often came from people who, as individuals, owed much to the charismatic movement and rejoiced in the renewal which it had brought to them.

Charismatic experiences and behaviour are fine in themselves: the problem is when they become a thing to belong to, over against the total community, in such a way that those who don't have this particular identity are made second-class citizens. The charismatic movement has made a great impact on white Anglicanism in South Africa in the last ten years. But Bishop Alphaeus Zulu had this phenomenon in a correct perspective when he said, 'We blacks have

111

never needed a charismatic *movement*; we've always been charismatic'. I think that this observation is quite justified. Black Anglicans have dutifully accepted the somewhat inflexible routines of Anglo-Catholic worship, and, I think, have usually found them genuinely interesting and meaningful; but outside the precise boundaries laid down by authority they have felt free to invent songs, to dance and yodel in open-air processions, and to sound the praise of God outside church after worship by fanfares on motor-horns. The rehearsed regularities of altar-boys' religion become absorbed into a more truly holy chaos, in which permissions and precedences are irrelevant and no one is made to feel unacceptable.

16 The Practice of Community

Any missionary endeavour has to ask itself: Is our programme having the effect of making people thank God that they are not as other men are, or is it having the effect of enabling them to rejoice that they are sharing in a purpose which is for all? It is hard for a minority movement not to want to be small and to justify itself by being different. It is right to want to be faithful: it is right to want to keep one's integrity unimpaired. And therefore it is right to recognize that our movement may not be popular or numerous. But that is very different to actually wishing to be exclusive.

So a very serious question arises about the process of exclusion. The Catholic movement, in Africa and Asia, has applied definite standards of church discipline. People have learned to value their 'church ticket', to get it signed each month when they receive communion and to get it signed each month when they pay their church dues. In spite of its alarming similarity to the pass system by which white minority governments regulate the lives of blacks, the church ticket seems to have been something of which its possessor was quite proud — although, in some cases, this may have been because of the risk of being denied a proper funeral if it was not up to date. The church ticket makes it clear what kind of membership the bearer has — catechumen, baptized person, communicant. And it also makes it clear whether the bearer is in good standing or is under suspension from communion.

All this seems worlds away from the vagueness of membership of the Church of England. Some of it is, of course, desirable in the case of a membership which may be largely illiterate and migratory. But what about the suspension from communion? In fact, the overwhelming majority of suspensions have been of women who get illegitimate babies, and for them the occasional span of time on the penitents' bench was a routine hazard. Neither the irregular pregnancy nor the suspension from communion caused them to stop coming to church and saying their prayers and believing in God. But the fact that this was virtually the only sin that was punished, and that this applied only to women, has brought the whole system of church discipline into disrepute: and so did the fact that it was a process which applied only among blacks — among whites, of course, 'bad girls' wouldn't want to go to church anyway! But church discipline is not just a stupid, old-fashioned idea. It is still needed. But its target ought to be those who offend the community by wanting the community to be unnecessarily and improperly exclusive. The Anglican Church's witness in Africa would have been more credible and coherent if it had imposed church discipline on a communicant who advocated and practised racial separation, and had been a bit less tough on a black woman who was a victim of a man's carelessness, or, for that matter, had simply satisfied her instinct for motherhood without the benefit of an authorized man.

Here, a church in a racially sensitive area could learn from the experience of a church in a village in North India, only about fifteen years ago. In this village a whole low-caste 'untouchable' community expressed its desire to become Christian. So some of the higher-caste church-members appealed to the rural dean (a USPG missionary), saying that unless these low-caste people went through a purification ceremony which would bring them up to the status of the upper-caste people, they would be unable to associate together in church or receive Communion together. The diocesan bishop (a high-caste man by birth) convened the diocesan executive to respond to this. (Part of the problem was that in those days, the local Roman Catholic church was providing just the sort of purification ceremony that was being asked for, for exactly this purpose.) The diocesan executive gave the matter lengthy attention; it eventually came out with a clear statement that caste discrimination is against the law of the church, and resolved that 'any member of the Anglican Church in this diocese who makes caste discrimination shall be excommunicated from the Christian fellowship until such time as he openly confesses his fault'. The executive appointed a team of fifteen people to go to the village concerned with a copy of the resolution and a letter from the bishop. All but a few members of the village church community accepted the decision; and those who did not, agreed to be excommunicated — most of these have since acknowledged their error and have been restored. A further effect of this was that the Roman Catholics gave up their purification ceremony. Here is a good example of a situation in which just to conform with local culture would have been destructive of community.

The Catholic instinct for recognizing and consecrating the natural order has very definite limits. It needs an aggressive critique in order to avoid a complacency that would bless the disorder within the natural order and that would connive with a divisive style of society. It is worth also noting how, even in small details, this story follows the pattern of that great model event in the Church's decision-making, the Council of Jerusalem, in Acts 15. Note particularly the advantage of having a chairman who is a natural conservative but is also genuinely alert to the new things that God is doing in the world. And, far too often, synods do their decision-making well, but fail to attend adequately to the need for sensitive publicity. Any church council or synod would do well to check its procedures, in detail, against the procedure followed in Acts 15.

I cannot evade an embarrassment at this point. Anglican Catholicism has often appeared to give the same answer to the non-episcopally confirmed as to the high-caste Indians gave to the low-caste Indians: 'We will accept you if you undergo a ceremony, episcopal confirmation, which will bring you up to our level.' We say that we have theologically justifiable reasons for our position; but we are certainly perceived as claiming that we are normal and that we will accept others only in terms of our normality. They have everything to gain and nothing to give. I am not convinced that, even if our theological arguments are correct, we are guiltless of a motive similar to that of the high-caste Indians.

The biggest danger of this whole approach to our relationships is, however, not just inter-denominational discourtesy: it is encouragement of the idea that the laity, in their different church traditions, are just receivers of the ministry of the specialists rather than active agents in mission in the world. But when a group of Christians of different denominations are working together in a costly confession out in the world, their identity is formed by their role in the world together, in the street or office-block or secular institution. Even the most Catholic-minded persons will feel that this frontier-situation is what gives them their calling, and not their ecclesiastical home-ground. Our church laws are made by ecclesiastical persons for whom the ecclesiastical system is home-ground; the tragedy is that these laws are shaped on the assumption that the ecclesiastical system is the lay-person's home-ground too: so the whole system gives the impression that a frontier situation is exceptional and that no ordinary lay-person will be found in it. It's at this point that the lay-person may well find that the only responsible action is one of responsible disobedience. This will not be carelessness about the doctrine of the Body of Christ: it will be recognition that the Body is most truly itself when it is out in the world, and that those who share in the work of the Body need to share, in some way, the sacramental life of the Body together. The doctrine of the Body is one of Catholicism's great treasures. It must be used to develop, not inhibit, the mission of the church. And indeed it has usually enabled Catholicism to stand for a responsible attitude to the implications of community in Christ.

Catholic Anglicanism has been right to insist on taking seriously the doctrine of the Body of Christ as the visible church. It has been able to resist the dangerous idea that there can be one church for the natives and one for the colonials. It has also been able to insist that church unity must be more than just a federation of friendly organizations.

It has been difficult to fit Anglicanism into the categories established by Protestant missiology: it has got no neat answer to the question, 'Where is your mission work?' It is full of blurred edges. The mission is part of the total work of the church; and, at least at the diocesan level, the 'mission' to the natives is part of the same structure as 'ministry' to expatriates or colonials. Catholicism has insisted that there must be one structure, as an evidence of the Body which is God's creation in Christ. Churches which have not held to this have had poor defences against the idea that we do not need to have any visible fellowship or any opportunity to love as brothers and sisters across colour and caste barriers. Without a vigorous commitment to such a doctrine, the answer can too easily be given that our fellowship is in heaven; and this answer perpetuates the disastrous misunderstanding that heaven is located on the far side of physical death.

There is a danger here, which Anglicanism has not entirely avoided. It is possible to offer a unity which is based on the most powerful culture — Englishness, or Latin-style ceremonial, or something of that sort. Uniformity is desirable, in order to avoid a sense of providing two standards. When a eucharistic text appeared called, 'A Liturgy for Africa', many Africans rejected it simply because the title suggested something racial and therefore second-rate. But a uniformity is almost bound to be the uniformity which is most acceptable to the most powerful group, and it is difficult to avoid this being a European imperialism. That which is English is international: that which is Ovambo is Ovambo. At a time when they are struggling to become part of the international world, black Namibians attach much importance to improving their English-language competence. This is a legitimate element in their striving for freedom. Africans are very wary of being given something 'ethnic' by their overlords; they, not unreasonably, suspect a stress on ethnic culture and tribal language as a device of the powerful to keep them divided. They don't mind identifying *themselves* as 'Bantu': but they object vigorously to being defined by the whites in such a term. One of the essential freedoms is a freedom not to be defined against one's will, and not to be limited by a definition imposed by the more powerful for their own purposes. So there is a continual tension between claiming one's own local inheritance and being part of a catholic unity.

In Southern Africa, on the whole, it has been the churches which have least valued the doctrine of the visible Body of Christ that have shown most enterprise in using local ethnic features in, for instance, their church architecture — but only in black areas and for black people! There is an illuminating contrast between two churches in Zululand. Lutherans have never had anything other than 'mission' work in Zululand: their congregations have been almost entirely Zulu, and where children of white Lutheran missionaries have stayed on in the area they have generally become Anglicans. Anglicans have for many years had a substantial white membership in southern Zululand; perhaps 10 per cent of the members of the diocese are white. The Lutheran church has, for a long time, conducted all its offical business in Zulu, and a white minister could not participate in the affairs of the church until he was competent in Zulu. The Anglican church allowed the language of the white minority to dominate, and its synods used to be conducted entirely in English. But, on the other hand, twenty-five years ago the Anglican Church had adopted a single stipend system for all its ministers, agreed by the synod, consisting of black and white members: only in the last decade has the Lutheran Church come, under pressure from its black members, to work out a stipend system that avoids big racial differentials. It is in these nuts-and-bolts issues that the meaning of community is given shape. It involves compromise at many points, and there is no ideal design.

It is important not to put so much value on a particular

type of community that those who cannot belong in such a community feel left out. For instance, for most of the Christian era, the church has had a picture of a settled community, a community identified with a particular area, with its own life-space. It has seen this as normal, and has sometimes attempted by means of special chaplaincies to meet the needs of those, like seamen, who do not fit this norm. But, for one reason or another, many do not fit this norm, and for them it is the geographically localized life that is abnormal.

There are those who are migrants. For them, home and work may be hundreds of miles apart, and life consists of a shuttling between the two. For some, the movement is traditional, caused by conditions of climate. For others, the movement is novel and more artificial, caused by regulations of politicians or employers. In the latter case, the church may well be in the forefront of the demand to have the conditions altered. But, even in such undesirable circumstances, the church has a main duty to see that migrants do not get the worst of both worlds, being treated as mere 'appendages' and not real members, both in the home church and in the church in the work area. Migrants have quite enough to cope with in any case. In particular, if they suffer injury and bring a law-suit against someone, they stand to lose their case simply because it can be deferred until their contract is over and they are no longer available to plead. But migrants can be agents of the creation of new community. The Anglican Church in Mozambique owes its origin not to European missionaries from far away but to black mineworkers on the Witwatersrand who were touched by Christian faith during their mine contract, and who took their faith home with them. And in a place like a mine compound, very rural and un-cosmopolitan men from a great variety of areas can meet and discover a fellowship that crosses divides of nationality and language, a fellowship of a common identity as a black working-class.

Similarly, the church needs to look with real respect on those whose way of life is nomadic. These are people for whom home and work are not far apart, but are never in

119

one place for very long. It is claimed that the Christian movement lost North Africa to Islam because it ceased to be a movement: it appealed to the settled people, at a time when nomadism was increasing due to the spread of the desert. Nomads generally have a bad image. Governments dislike them, because they make nonsense of national boundaries and cause endless problems for educators and census officials. They have often been blamed for ruining the land. In fact, however, there is a certain kind of land which is more fertile than desert but too poor for settled occupation. A settled population would turn it into desert by overgrazing, and a total absence of population would turn it into desert by depriving it of manure. The nomads fill this place in the ecological picture: and it is up to the church to encourage them to do so and not to make them feel that they can't be Christians simply because they don't fit into the parish system.

In South America, a mission agency set up a mission station on a river where people had traditionally supported themselves by fishing up and down a stretch of a hundred miles or more. The located static character of the mission made people feel that if they wanted to take Christianity seriously they had to stay within easy reach of the mission. And so they stopped living as nomads, and what used to be a balanced use of the river's resources has been abandoned.

The Anglican Church in Namibia had an opportunity about twenty years ago to establish itself among a nomadic community in the Kaokoveld, a semi-desert area in the north-west of the territory. A man called Thomas Ruhozu walked two hundred miles from the community to join the Anglican school at Odibo. He stayed there as a pupil for four years, and was baptized and confirmed. Then his father died, and he returned to look after the cattle. Nothing more happened for a few years: then a member of the diocesan staff in Windhoek wrote a letter to Thomas Ruhozu, to ask if he knew any other Anglicans in that area. He got no letter in reply; instead, six weeks later, Mr Ruhozu turned up at Windhoek in person, having travelled six hundred miles from the Kaokoveld. It was clear that the government was making it almost impossible for ordinary diocesan priests to visit that area; so, for the two weeks that he could stay in Windhoek he was given a crash course in Christian ministry. He then went home. He was given some money to cover expenses, and to rent a post-office box in the main town in the Kaokoveld, which he might be able to visit every two months or so. Six weeks later an archdeacon from the northern part of the diocese was able to get across to see how he was faring, and was presented with eleven people to be admitted as catechumens. Two months later these were baptized; but on a subsequent visit, the archdeacon could not find Mr Ruhozu and his colleagues, as their nomadic life had taken them off into another part of the district. There were plans to give Mr Ruhozu further training and to ordain him: this was clearly the right answer, as a priest from two hundred miles away could not possibly keep track of a nomadic people. This programme was interrupted by deportations and other government interference with the diocesan staff, and by the increasing obstacles put in the way of anyone wishing to visit the Kaokoveld.

For the real growth of the church in a nomadic group, it must avoid being too long dependent on the expertize of even the most sympathetic outsider. The problem then is for the central settled church to make sure that the leadership of the nomad church is kept as fully in touch as possible; and the 'normal' church must give itself a chance to learn from what is happening in the nomad church's experience.

And in case this should all seem specialized and distant, may we ask how far established Anglicanism in England has succeeded in relating to gypsies?

What is the ideal size for a church community? For the church to be catholic, it must be large enough to have within it reasonable variety. People can claim to be very keen on the idea of community, when all that they really mean is that they like the little clique of exiles or enthusiasts to which they belong. Such a 'community' will have well-marked and narrow limits. At the same time, for the church to be catholic, in the sense of being able to make its special contribution to the whole people of God, it must be small enough to be local. People can claim to be keen on catholicity, when what they really mean is that they like to have a pretext to be escapees from the particularity of their own place and area. Catholicism has been much better at providing answers in terms of what is decreed by a distant, external authority than in working out what is really needed in the local context.

Community is, therefore, pulled in opposite directions. And both are needed. The real skill of Catholicism should be in enabling the local church to be genuinely local, without losing its participation in something bigger. Paul's doctrine of the Body starts with the whole and works down to the parts. The one Body is the starting-point; the variety is necessary and possible because of the unity. The Body becomes its members; it does not come into being through the coming-together of separate elements. To start from the variety means that movement has to be inwards, towards more intense unity. That picture has its value: but the sounder picture is to start from the unity and to move out into 'variety' which need have no limit.

There have been many attempts to work out the implications of this. One such was a system devised by the Presbyterian Church in Taiwan during a period of rapid growth. They established a rule that any church which grew larger than forty-five adults should consider itself to be large enough, and should split to enable the church to be more local. Churches used sometimes to apologize for having allowed themselves to grow too large. Clearly, a procedure of this kind helps people to feel that they are, individually, part of a working team. At the same time, a church which is as local as this, at least in an urban area, may well miss the variety of social type and class that is needed for catholicity. Unless it retains a sense of mission, it will become cosy. It is vital not to confuse community with homogeneity.

In fact, Catholic doctrine insists that membership of Christian community is based in grace and is marked by baptism. It is not a company of those who have chosen each other: it does not consist of those who have graduated by either social or moral or intellectual or cultural degrees. To be Catholic means to accept those whom God gives to us, not just those of whose opinions, behaviour or smell we happen to approve. This is bound to be difficult. We have to acknowledge that God did not design our neighbour as we would like our neighbour to be. What is more, God has not made his church to fit in with our dreams, even our dreams of justice and peace. Those who yearn for change in the church have to make sure that they are not more in love with their fantasy of the church than they are with the awkward real-life brothers and sisters who are actually given by God to be church to us. Those who are reckoned to be 'prophetic' have to be on their guard that they do not take their prophetic role as a licence to give sanctuary to unrecognized hatreds or as a way of limiting their human contacts to people with whom they can feel a natural togetherness.

A church in a white, middle-class suburb of a city like Johannesburg may feel quite a strong sense of togetherness, but only because it has screened so many types of people out. The same applies to the kind of seminaries which have been generated by the party system within the Church of England. Any church or Christian organization which prides itself on being 'friendly' should ask, what price our friendliness? Who is being excluded? Who is not represented? If churches find it easy to gather together into a covenanted relationship, one reason may be that they are all pretty similar already — not necessarily in doctrine but in social make-up and general attitude. And then God will have to let new churches be raised up to represent the prayer and the yearning of the misfit, the leper, the stranger.

One of the most helpful remarks which I have heard was an almost throw-away comment by Albert van den Heuvel during a visit to South Africa, when he was Youth Secretary of the World Council of Churches. After a long meeting with students who were deeply concerned about their role in church and society, he said: 'It is one of the marks of the Gospel that it does not abolish conflict but it converts conflict into tension.' This is abundantly true about the conflict of interest between the local church and the more inclusive church, in the search for community. The two need each other. I have to testify to the continuing validity of the mission strategy which was developed by Ernie Southcott and his parish community in Leeds in the 1950s. Critics used to accuse him of wanting to replace the parish church by the house church. This is a fair criticism of some house-church groups in more recent years, which seem to exist because their members are alienated from or are refugees from the parish churches. But it was not a fair criticism of the 'Halton experiment'. There, they were quite clear that the house church and the parish church needed each other. Without the parish church, the house church would be a single-class semi-private adventure with no power to reconcile across the massive social divides of the area. Without the house church, the parish church would provide a non-local, non-rooted religious club which would be next-door to no one in particular. The church has to exist by continual expansion and contraction, alternating gatheredness with scatteredness, recognizing that (despite some modern translations) Paul meant what he said when he used the same word 'church' to describe the people of God throughout the world, the people of God in the city of Corinth, and the people of God in the house of Nymphas.

That vision of a multiform church, a community of both localness and universalness, a household of welcoming openness and cherishing closeness, is a realistic practical programme for a church-in-mission. It was no accident that one of our guiding principles was derived from a leader of the overseas church — none other than Bishop Frank Weston; he taught that local mission depends on developing the right relationship between the two communities, the congregation and the parish — the 'parish' in the strict meaning of the total population of the area. In the last thirty years, there has been quite a lot of development within just two areas of the whole scene — the ecumenical and the liturgical — but, otherwise, Ernie Southcott's vision, rooted in a vigorous eucharistic Catholicism, remains as critical and creative as ever. Much of it has not really been taken on board in our churches; but I have found that its central convictions have continued to make sense in every place where I have myself sought to exercise a ministry.[35]

17 The Church as an International Community

The church has to take structure seriously, because structure is the method by which spirit is embodied. No amount of goodwill and friendly talk can compensate for the fact that the churches are structured as if they were a series of competitive clubs. And when community is to happen on any scale wider than the most local scale, some kind of structure has to be brought into being; and we have to test whether it expresses or denies the community ideal which it is supposed to represent.

Both *Essays Catholic and Missionary* (1928) and *Catholic Anglicans Today* (1968) were heavily preoccupied with problems of church unity and intercommunion. In the latter volume, Fr Gibbard's essay on 'Catholics in the World Church' is almost completely limited to this sort of issue. He starts with the excellent remark, 'To be a Catholic is to be committed to ecumenical action and thus to enduring a situation of anomalies and risks.'[36] This kind of insight has helped many Anglican Catholics to overcome their hesitations about the ecumenical movement. In a way which I think would not have been possible thirty years ago, many of us would feel that it is totally and splendidly appropriate that the 150th anniversary of the start of our tradition should coincide so closely with the Vancouver Assembly of the World Council of Churches.

Of course, the kind of ecumenism of which Fr Gibbard wrote is still required — the recent history of church relations in Britain demonstrates as much — but the situation has changed. In most of India, Anglicanism as such is a thing of the past; it has yielded its identity into 'united churches'. In much of Africa, the situation is quite different. Africans seem to see relatively little disadvantage and scandal in the existence of a variety of traditions, provided that they are not used as ways of excluding people. In belonging to a particular church, they say, I am not limiting myself or condemning others: I can be catholic and evangelical and charismatic, within one skin.

A further reason for a certain decline in the urgency of the inter-church question is that it looks rather domestic and frivolous compared to what many would feel is the really ecumenical question now, a question which cuts across all traditions. The old question was, 'Can the non-episcopally confirmed share in communion with those who are episcopally confirmed?' The new question is 'Can the poor share in communion with those who make them poor?' And, because the boundaries between rich and poor lie between nations as well as within nations, this urgently affects any international Christian organization, such as a missionary society.

'Missionary, go home' was a plea from the poor to the rich. We cannot be a church until you stop dominating us with your wealth, structures and assumptions. In the days of *Essays Catholic and Missionary* this demand seems to have come mainly from India. In the early 1970s it was coming from Africa. The key word was 'moratorium': both sending and receiving churches were being told to take painful action to end the era of dependency. The demand was not without effect. The number of Anglicans going overseas as missionaries in the traditional sense (especially through the United Society for the Propagation of the Gospel) declined quite sharply. What is perhaps more important, it became far more common for British missionaries to go overseas for very short periods, of three years or so, rather than as a life long commitment. Moratorium was not the only reason for this; but it was impossible to disguise the sense that the market for overseas missionaries was closing up. USPG continued to receive roughly the same number of initial enquiries as in the past, from people interested in exploring the possibility of mission service, but a smaller proportion eventually went overseas. USPG's Association of Missionary Candidates changed itself into Christians Aware, a group concerned with a wide range of issues in mission, in Britain and in the world as a whole, rather than just with fostering vocations to overseas mission in the traditional sense.

Moratorium, as such, had a short life. It always meant more to the professional African church worker than it did to the ordinary church member: by the mid-1970s few ordinary church members of any churches in Africa except the Roman Catholics would have had much consciousness of dependence on overseas resources of either staff or money. That's not to say that these resources are now negligible; far from it. But they are of the kind which are most observed by central church officials rather than by ordinary members. And the great expansion of Christianity in Africa has been almost entirely led by Africans.

The pattern started to change as the decade drew to a close. The number of missionaries going overseas through USPG started to rise. The Elective Assembly of the Diocese of Central Zambia found itself inviting an elderly and courageous white Archbishop to come out of retirement to be its bishop. And a shift has developed in the kind of work which the missionary is asked to do. The church-worker from overseas may be invited, not do a job which no local person can do, but to do a job which already has been done by a local person. A missionary of this kind is valued not primarily in order to bring an expertize which is otherwise not available but to bring an international catholicity into the whole church's team. In such circumstances, the local leaders have lost much of their anxiety about dependency and are no longer afraid that whites may dominate them. This is a maturity which has been true of work in the Caribbean for some time, and is now affecting much work in Africa as well. And this makes it possible to recognize that a church which, through no fault of its own, has been deprived of missionary staff — such as the church in Burma — is truly a poor church, not because it is short of Western expertize but because it is not nourished by the explorers, the internationalists, the odd characters who come in from outside under the label of 'missionary'.

Patterns of dependency shift. One of the biggest growth-areas in USPG's work has been in the bringing of overseas nationals to Britain for specialist training and for parochial experience. When this enterprise, which is shared with most of the major missionary societies, is added to the rapid growth in diocesan ventures of the same kind, it becomes a very considerable development in inter-church relations. If there is a new form of dependency to beware of, it would be the notion that an overseas church's problems can be solved by sending someone to Britain. There can be an unfortunate class-distinction overseas between those who have 'been-to' and those who haven't. None the less, this development should now be seen as one of the most important contributions which a missionary society can make, especially when those who come for specialist training go back home to help to make that same specialist training available in their own areas. Mission agencies are careful to ensure that, when they bring an overseas student to Britain, they are not depriving an institution of further education in Africa or Asia of a potential student. This is one reason, apart from the appalling increase in costs, for refusing to bring people to Britain for ordinary university courses.

A Catholic understanding of mission will see mission as a function of the church and not as a thing-in-itself. This is essential to the right functioning of a missionary society. After nearly six years as a senior staff-member of USPG, I have to say that (and I hope I may be forgiven for the apparent churlishness of this remark) I neither know nor do I particularly care who actually are the members of the Society. What does matter to me very much is that the Society does not make its missionaries members of itself: it sends them overseas to be members of the local church, to identify with it, to find fellowship within it, to be paid according to its salary scales, and to take part in its internal politics. When I was a USPG missionary overseas, I was actually aware of USPG for about six hours a year — the time that it took me to write my annual statement. Otherwise, all my identity was with the church to which the Society had sent me.

Having said that, I acknowledge, that, in all sorts of detailed ways, especially at the beginning and the end of a tour of mission duty overseas, USPG gives a great deal of individual support to its missionaries. In some ways this increases as the number of mission agents overseas is reduced. And before anyone starts muttering 'Parkinson', I think that it's fair to say that in some ways it is more difficult for a European to go into the 'Third World' today than it used to be. The gap in 'standard of living' between Britain and, say, Tanzania has widened; the more you are used to having, the greater the sacrifice. Most of the other whites going to such places go in the service of governments or multi-national corporations, with remuneration levels which make today's missionaries comparatively poorer than their forebears. Missionaries from the USA and from the European mainland tend to have greater financial backing, too. (Some of them have found our conditions at Selly Oak a bit austere for their liking, so we suggest that they might see the relative poverty of Britain as a half-way house in preparation for Malawi or Bangladesh.) So it is certainly right for a society to take personal care of its missionaries, provided that by doing so it does not compromise too much its commitment to the overseas church itself.

If the missionary society makes itself very important in the consciousness of its missionaries, particularly in the early days of their recruitment and training, it will doubtless succeed in giving them a sense of membership of a committed and sacrifical community. And that is very valuable. But they need, somehow, to leave that sense of membership at the airport when they depart for their posting. Otherwise, the precious community of discipleship in Britain will turn into a white clique of expatriates overseas: all sorts of differentials of work and life-style will distinguish the expatriate community from the native church. There will be little chance for community, as such, to be seen as a creation of the Gospel. This is one of the most searching critiques offered to us by our African and Asian colleagues.

Can the missionary society be a religious community itself, as some would wish it to be? Or, what is the place of the religious community within the totality of mission? Wherever it has gone overseas, Catholic Anglicanism has taken a sense of the value of the religious community. The great Anglican communities in England — such as the Community of St Mary the Virgin, the Order of the Holy Paraclete, the Society of St John the Evangelist, the Community of the Resurrection, and many more — have responded to requests to put their resources to work overseas, and have done so with great commitment. Others, like the Society of the Sacred Mission, were actually born in a vocation to overseas mission. Their contribution has been an essential part of the history of the dioceses to which they were sent, because so often they were able to provide the resources to initiate institutions which no other agency could attempt to provide. If there is a weakness, it would be that sometimes the sheer scale of what they developed has made it difficult to hand on their work to the local church.

In the long run, the religious communities seem to have two special values in the mission areas to which they have gone — and these apply to the contribution of all communities, whether contemplative or active. First, in some cases at least, they have been a sign that native and expatriate really can live on a level together, with a common rule, common purse, common sharing of menial jobs. When a missionary society can do this, then it can indeed claim to be a religious community. Secondly, and more generally, where a church moves into an area with a religious community as part of its team — or even as part of its ideal — it can convey to the indigenous Christians that some sort of community enterprise may be part of their calling. In the long run, the communities for which 'Third World' Anglicanism should be most grateful are those which have been inspired within the 'Third World' itself, whether they be English-inspired, like Frank Weston's Community of the Sacred Passion, or more totally indigenous, like the Melanesian Brotherhood founded by Ini Kopuria.[37] And the churches in Britain have cause to be thankful for the overseas involvement of the religious communities. When other missionaries return from overseas service to Britain, they get distributed all over the church. This is all to the good, and it is no doubt of advantage to churches up and down the country. But communities like the Community of the Resurrection and the Community of St Mary the Virgin hold together substantial continuing groups of ex-missionaries, combining long experience of overseas areas, and these can provide a significant Southern African or Far Eastern presence within the British Church. And the Community of the Sacred Passion, in setting up its little group of nuns in a council house in an ordinary street in Walsall, has brought to Britain some of the discipline of living simply and of living really close to the people, which it has developed in its home-area in Tanzania.

Catholicity means being in community with people different from yourself. The churches in Britain have been sending their values to the ends of the earth. In this era, the flow is becoming two-way, and the missionary societies are best-placed to be agents of this process. The development of overseas provinces is stimulating the demand for church-to-church relationships. In many cases, an overseas province includes areas influenced by and related to both the major Anglican missionary societies, the United Society for the Propagation of the Gospel and the Church Missionary Society — two societies which differ widely from each other in style, administration, and tradition — as well as to societies which relate to more specific areas. From these provinces, we can expect an increasing impatience with the way in which responsibility for overseas mission is organized within British Anglicanism.

The missionary societies are examples of the extra-ordinary voluntary character of British institutional life, which brings upon us not only the scorn of critical Marxists but also the almost angry incomprehension of otherwise gentle and friendly Scandinavians. At its worst, this system means that most of the real resources are not at the disposal of the church's official decision-making bodies but are controlled by sectional interest-groups which are not answerable to the church as a whole: it means, also, that the Church of England has not been able to move to the more theologically sound position of the Episcopalians in the USA, who insist that the church itself is the missionary society and itself fulfils all the necessary functions of a missionary society. At its best, the British system provides informal organizations which can act more quickly and freely than the official establishment: also, USPG and CMS are not based only in the Church of England but in British Anglicanism as a whole. They do not have to look to examples 3,000 miles away to find Anglicanism in a non-established mode, for they have it in their own structures, in the churches in the Celtic nations; and, through them, the overseas churches can relate to something a good deal wider than the Church of England.

The Church of England has been very slow in accepting the idea that, at an official and structural level, it can benefit from the critique of persons from outside itself. It is open to the accusation that it is willing to send people to evangelize others but does not like the idea of being evangelized itself. Be that as it may, England is almost the last of the areas of Anglicanism to accept a Partners-in-Mission consultation; and this consultation could scarcely have taken place at all without the pressure and the contributions of the missionary societies. In the end, some of the fears of the critics may have been proved true, and part of the report of the consultation is erratic and contradictory.

On the theme of the church's community-life, for instance, I find it difficult to believe that anyone with experience of diocesan life in Africa or Asia could agree with the conviction expressed in the report that every parish should be wholly responsible for all its costs.[38] Part of the essentially Anglican understanding of community is that a region, rather than a very local area, should be the main administrative unit, and that within that region there should be a corporate sharing-out of both resources and responsibilities. In a country where there is an inequitable sharing-out of wealth, the church connives with the existing conditions if it insists that each parish has to be financially self-sufficient. The only way to ensure that would be to spread the pastoral care much more thinly in poor areas than in rich areas, and there is enough tendency in that direction already without it being encouraged by an international consultation. But if the financial unit is the diocese, there is some chance of overcoming at least the local inequities.

The Church of England and the Church in Wales have now both experienced Partners-in-Mission consultations, the former in 1981 and the latter in 1978. In each case, a team from outside the province or provinces concerned came and lived for a short time in the area, and then shared evaluations in very intensive consultative meetings. I have, I'm sorry to say, picked out what seems to me to be one poor judgement in the Church of England document; this is unfair to the report as a whole, which shows a great deal of insight into the peculiar character of the Church of England. The Church in Wales report is less complex, less inspiring, but more practical, and many of its recommendations could be transposed without much difficulty into an overseas context.

But the question which should concern us here is, how are our churches in Britain to gain from our international community? How are we to make the most of our catholicity? The most serious criticism of the Partners-in-Mission programme is that we are asking visiting partners to do exactly what we tell missionaries not to do, namely to descend on an area and make their evaluations before they have had time really to belong. There is a problem, of course. If you stay too long, you lose the criteria which you bring from outside, and you then assimilate, as far too many Christian expatriates, including priests, have done in Southern Africa. To those who say, 'You can't understand us unless you have lived here for X years' (a very common defence by white South Africans), it is surely right to reply with the story of the man who went into a pub at 10.15 p.m. and complained that it was stuffy, and got the reply, 'Who are you to say it's stuffy, you've only just arrived?'

For really helpful evaluation, however, we need more than initial impressions and comparisons with back home. I wonder if there has been any attempt to co-ordinate the perceptions of serious visitors from overseas who have stayed for a longer time than the Partners-in-Mission consultants? There is an increasing number of such people, some of them students, some of them people on experience exchange, some of them migratory or not-so-migratory workers. The missionary societies are doing much to improve the international catholicity of British Christianity by facilitating visits of between six and twelve months: these are the people who could, perhaps, help us in a different kind of partnership project. In some cases, as in the project where an exceptionally perceptive Zulu priest came to stay in a rural area of the Diocese of Hereford, such schemes are consciously set up as part of a programme of mission-in-Britain.

The catholicity of sharing wealth within a diocese needs to be translated into wider terms, and the missionary society is the obvious agent for this. Most missionary giving has been done in response to particular appeals. We give to a 'good cause'. We trust that the money will be spent well, and we expect the collecting agency to see that it is. But this is the way of the powerful. We use money to get things done which we think should be done, because fundamentally we believe that the money is ours. The New Testament knows of no such system. The only collections which are referred to in the Acts and Epistles were taken because one group had more than another. There was an inequitable distribution of wealth, and within the fellowship of the church this inequality was rectified. Within the province of Southern Africa, for instance, it is obvious that the *per capita* wealth of Lesotho is far lower than that of the Southern Transvaal, because the wealth generated by the

Basuto migrant mineworkers is mainly retained within the mining area. So, if the Diocese of Johannesburg sends money to the Diocese of Lesotho, it isn't 'charity': it is a paying to the poor of what would have been paid to them if the system were not so unjust. In that circumstance, you don't ask what the recipient is going to do with the money, any more than you check what an employee is going to do with his wage. The recipient may use it for a creche, or she may blow it on a party.

On a wider scale, the churches in Malaŵi and Bangladesh are poor. They find it difficult to provide for many of the basic necessities of church life. But why? They are poor because their members are poor: the members are poor because the countries themselves are poor: the countries are themselves poor, partly because we are in a world-system where the primary producers get least reward. What, then, is the role of the missionary society? To collect money to buy hymn books in Chichewa and Bengali and send them out? To send cash direct, without strings, to the poor peasants in Malaŵi and Bangladesh — and that might mean somehow by-passing the official church channels and sending money to the poorest women in the villages, perhaps by means of a new kind of Mothers' Union network? Or to use its resources entirely within Britain and the northern hemisphere, to bring pressure on those whose decisions affect the market value of the products of the poor world?

The missionary societies are seeing that the decision on this kind of matter must be made by the churches in partnership, and not just by the churches which, by the luck of the economic system, happen to be the immediate source of funds. The money which the societies have at their disposal fundamentally belongs to the overseas churches. So, USPG now insists that the group which does the basic decision-making on budgetary policy must include a substantial proportion of overseas church representatives.

And the poorer churches are having to face new questions, such as: 'You used to think that missionaries cost you nothing — indeed, you used to think that they could do work for you free which otherwise you would have to pay

136

for yourself. Now you see that for the cost of sending one missionary we might be able to finance two or more local workers: which do you want, expatriate staff or the money to do the job yourself?'

Compared with the funds handled by international corporations and governments, the resources of the churches and their missionary societies are tiny. But they represent the old biblical truth that any true community must include a community of goods. In our insignificance, we are the priests of creation, because we present an alternative to the conventional assumption that creation is a source of weapons whereby human beings can exploit each other. Money and things are body, part of the one body broken for all.

PEOPLE IN MISSION

18   The Missionary

So, who is going to be this community of confrontation and proclamation, of healing and truth, in these days?

In one sense, the most important sense, there is no difference between now and fifty or a hundred and fifty years ago. The Gospel will be commended by those for whom Jesus makes living sense, and who take seriously the implications of the revelation that God works through a Body. The missionary character has to be a character of faith — faith as a mixture of security and adaptability. The test of the Catholic faith is whether it can go on nurturing this kind of character. In principle, Catholicism is certainly well-fitted for developing this kind of character — but it cannot be the kind of Catholicism which sends people anxiously looking around for churches which suit them or which measure up to precise cultural standards.

Today's Catholic missionary, in Britain or overseas, has to be someone who can sit light to many matters of religious expression, and who can live alongside Christians — and others — whose practices and expressions of belief are unfamiliar and perhaps uncongenial, and yet hold firmly to the basic reason for being there. Catholicism, if it is true to its nature, encourages us to delight in variety of language, of imagery, of ways of seeing things. It does not merely tolerate these differences; it sees them as essential to its own vision of unity. It affirms the uniqueness of the Gospel of Christ, but insists that this uniqueness is based in a design of inclusiveness, not of exclusiveness. It discovers and demonstrates how 'all things relate to the one central point of redemption and healing'.[39] This is what the Catholic sacramental tradition, at its most characteristic, encourages in those who learn from it. A healthy tradition needs to be 'like a skeleton, inside the body, giving it strength, not outside, like the hard shell of a crab, holding the life in'.[40] Unamuno made this searching distinction as a member of the minority Basque nation, but it is a highly relevant test for the tradition of any small and self-conscious group or community. There is something fundamentally contrary to the central character of Catholicism, when the badges or insignia of Catholicism are valued primarily as a means of telling us who is a Catholic — or 'a proper Catholic' — and who is not. The marks of Catholicism are then being used for an anti-catholic purpose. And the same applies, even more, to Christianity itself. Christian mission is best served not by those who are skilled at defining the boundaries but by those who are so held by the central truth that the boundaries become irrelevant — with the one massive proviso that the 'central truth' is not just a statement, or a vision, or a theory, or a doctrine, but a community of people acting the truth as the Body of Christ.

So we look for people with faith, with a fundamental personal security in Christ and in Christ's purposes, and therefore with a complete openness in everything else. How does one find people like this, or how does one form such people?

In the Department of Mission at Selly Oak, and in its four participant colleges, the British churches and missionary societies have a unique ecumenical instrument where British, Continental and 'Third World' Christians learn and train together for mission service. The tradition of the Department is formed by the primary task of preparing British people for service in the 'Third World': but it is much truer to the real nature of mission in the contemporary world to see it as mission in six continents. In practice, with the increasing number of British people going overseas for short periods, the Department is very clear that, in most cases, the British people who are trained there are going to be doing most of their active mission service in Britain, after their overseas tour is over.

In 1977, the Department published a long and carefully-worded statement of Aim and Objective, partly so as to interpret its nature to the churches, but mainly so as to work out a basis for its own curriculum. This statement is a useful account of what is necessary for practitioners in mission, so I will quote parts of it in full.

Aim

The aim of the course is to enable participants to assist as effective agents of Christian mission in the community in which they are to serve, whatever their task and wherever it may be.

Objective

To this end, the objective of the course is to help students to understand and to accept for themselves the implications of commitment to Jesus Christ as Lord of all creation and within all cultures, in proclamation of the Gospel, in seeking God's Kingdom and justice within the contemporary world, and in sharing in the life, witness, and renewal of the churches to which they are sent. [Note the stress here on the place of the receiving church, under whose authority the work has to be done.]

Then follows a series of ten items in the programme of learning for which opportunity will be provided within the course, including biblical, theological, sociological, anthropological, historical and linguistic studies; study of the faiths, cultures and religious systems which operate in the modern world (including capitalism and Marxism); communication studies; studies of the various areas for which students are destined; and a chance for students to relate their faith to their professional work. These are all, more or less, class-room or seminar types of learning. But then we on the staff asked ourselves: In our actual practice of mission, what were the skills and abilities which we ourselves found we most needed? What were the forms of knowledge, the presence or absence of which could either make or break a church-in-mission? And we found that we came up with a rather different kind of list, and we felt that these were so important that we had to include them, even if we couldn't see how they could be incorporated into any ordinary kind of educational curriculum. So there developed item 11, which takes the risk of saying:

. . . the programme of learning will include opportunities for participants to grow as men and women in Christ, and in particular

(a) to grow in their experience and practice of prayer, worship, and discipleship.

(b) to broaden their awareness of the Christian traditions of spirituality.

(c) to identify and celebrate what is good and true in the created order.

(d) to appropriate the resources of Christ's atonement and resurrection in handling conflict and guilt, including corporate guilt.

(e) to be willing to live in frontier situations, without familiar landmarks, and to be prepared to experience alienation.

(f) to be sensitive to the spiritual problems involved in making decisions, especially in times of crisis, and in identifying what must be abandoned and what must be retained.

(g) to handle questions of their own successes and failures with the resources of the Christian Gospel, to define their own particular needs and to seek out the resources to meet them.

Most of what the Department tries to provide, it provides well; it fulfils its aim. This item, I'm sure it does badly: it gets nowhere near fulfilling its aim. But to try this and to fail is more important than to try the rest and to succeed. If a thing is worth doing, it's worth doing badly! And when students are asked what, out of all the items offered, they think they most need, they often give highest priority to this item, especially to sections c, d, and e.

Perhaps the best outline for mission training is the process described in the opening paragraphs of Mark's gospel. Notice four movements of development in the experience of Jesus:

1   He identifies himself with a movement of repentance; he joins something which already is there, a movement of social criticism and of hope, a movement which is looking for change. He belongs in it. He lives within the convention of his culture, he goes down into its water, into its mud. He accepts the authority of the existing leadership.

2   He is affirmed, given an assurance of his value; he is claimed, identified, and blessed by the Spirit; and this happens on the far side of his descent into the water, as he climbs out dripping from his immersion into the common identity of John the Baptist's movement.

3   Immediately after this commissioning, he is sent off, not into his work but into the desert: he goes to be alone, to learn the discipline of independence — which means the ability to make decisions which are valid in themselves and not because they promote his own support-group or because they save him from isolation.

4   He waits until there is a suitable opening into which he can move, an opening caused in this instance by the police-action against John. He claims that a new opportunity has come; those who want to take advantage of it should join him. He goes out looking for colleagues. He finds them, as we have already observed, not among the people who are established in social influence but among people on the edges of society.

Jesus starts with the marginal and provincial people of Galilee; he takes people from there with him to the big city. The peasants know him before the cosmopolitans do. The same programme is followed in Acts; the church moves from the edge of the Empire to the centre. The Gospel can properly be heard only when the powerful are able to attend to the testimony of the less powerful.

142

From these elements in the experience of Jesus, let us observe four guidelines for people starting in mission service:

1 Mission, by definition, means moving into a situation which is bad, and living creatively within it. The most testing problems for any new missionary are: 'How far do I identify? At what speed do I move? How do I get into a bad situation without becoming compromised and contaminated by it?' And the answer has to be: Until you are in it, immersed in it, you won't be able to make any move at all. But you will probably be able to find a John-figure — not necessarily a worshipping group, but a person or persons who have some sense of a need and of an opportunity for change. Find this 'John-group'. Join in, build on it; perhaps, even, take it over, but not by being a rival to the existing leadership or by setting up in opposition. Movements of radical criticism are quite vulnerable enough without being torn apart by personality-cults. Anyway, you are to belong in the scene to which you are sent. And you will almost certainly find things in it which seem to you to be strange or wrong.

For instance, you may well find, if you go to a mission posting overseas, that the whole set-up seems to be much more authoritarian than what you are used to — particularly if you have never belonged to a trade union or if you are used to the individualism of the Church of England ministry. Well, perhaps it *is* authoritarian: perhaps there are junior members of the church staff and menial workers who are exploited and stunted. But you are not going to be able to do any good within such a situation until you have taken a place within that authoritarian system, until you are sufficiently alongside the exploited as to be able to speak with them and not instead of them; then you will be able to speak from the experience which is theirs and not just your imagination.

Or, as another example of something which may seem strange to you as you go into a new situation, you may find yourself closely relating to a church which gives much more recognition to women in the ministry than you are used to, and has them celebrating the eucharist or acting as prophetic church leaders. You may find that, if there is opposition to women serving as priests, it won't be on the grounds that you are used to arguing about — the grounds that in Europe would be called 'theological' — but on grounds which you might want to call 'cultural', such as that local tradition reserves the role of sacrifice-maker to males. But then, you will acknowledge that this was true in the old Israel also, and that Christ comes to the traditional cultures of both Israel and Africa as critic, at many points, and as the enlarger of boundaries. So you may find yourself drawn to the sense that the judgements which you previously brought to this particular matter were far more culturally conditioned than you had realized.

In both these instances, as in many others, you will not be able to come to a judgement until you belong. And the you that has started to belong will be a different you. You enter the convention, participate in it, and then begin to make your contribution. You may find, as I have done, great value in Jung's remark: 'Creative life is always on the yonder side of convention.'[41]

2   At some stage, a voice of authority outside yourself gives you a commissioning. You are affirmed and valued. You go. You don't necessarily know what you are going to do. In the first instance, you don't go to do anything. You don't go to achieve anything. You go to be a person who has been affirmed and valued by God; you go as one who is secure in God's love, who is confident of access to the Father, who can therefore risk failure and non-achievement, because your value does not depend on any achievement of yours but on the relationship which the Father has made with you. This freedom from the compulsion to succeed is itself a sign of the manner of God's remedy for the world. You are free to fail, free to be crucified and therefore to be raised from death.

3   You go into the desert. You go to a place where there are no flowers, no landmarks, and no company. You go to

learn to be alone, so that when you do have an opportunity to be a creator of community you do not create community only in order to rescue yourself from loneliness. You go to recognize the ways in which motives make their appeal to you. You go to learn to live in the real world and to detect the offers of self-regarding fantasy (specimens are given in the more extended accounts of this phase in Luke's and Matthew's gospels). You go to learn to be content with silence: in your mission, your greatest danger (especially if you are good with words) may well be your desire to fill every space with talk. Unless you can cope with empty space, you will leave nothing for your neighbour to fill. Then, your ignorance will be your own fault, for you will have not allowed yourself an opportunity to listen. And if you can't listen to your sister whom you have seen, how do you expect to listen to God whom you have not seen? (see I John 4:20).

Every missionary candidate, by the grace of God, will experience the desert in some way. For some, it comes after the fuss and excitement of being welcomed in the new area. For others, it takes the form of months of uncertainty about acceptance, about future work or destination, about visas and work-permits and so on. For others, the desert is the experience of the training institution. No college staff would actually want to organize their college to be a desert; but I think that it's much better that students should look back to the college as a desert than that they should look back to it, from a tough and barren place overseas, with nostalgia, as a kind of heaven in the past.

So, when students complain, as they sometimes do, about details of the course, and give the staff low marks for the organizing and presenting of material, or for the structure and community-life of the college, staff do have the right to ask in reply, What sort of marks do you give to yourself for your ability to bring about change, to improve, to take something unsatisfactory and make something useful out of it — for these are the abilities you are going to need in your mission work?

4 Where are you going to find your colleagues, your ways into society? Our normal conventions, both in Europe and elsewhere, say: Go to where the power is; bring about change there, and this will affect the conditions and opportunities for those lower down the social ladder; if you start at any other level, the powerful will cut you off before you can really get going at all. But the Christian movement is not one more movement among other movements. It starts from the other end. Indeed, the powerful tried to kill it; but crucifixion was its real start, and the law could not prove it guilty. We do not depend, for our success, on the processes which put other people into the 'successful' positions; we do not have to be expensively served with all the latest information; we do not have to have the equipment which will make other people admirers and enviers rather than brothers and sisters.

Indeed, one of the real changes in the last fifty years, which is reflected all over the place in our training programme, is that there is no longer a 'profession' called 'missionary'. There is no specific professional identity, job-specification, career-pattern, advancement-system and so on. To be a missionary means to do the job you are already doing, but to do it in a particular context. The training that is needed is not pre-service training; it is in-service training, to assist people who already have some specific skills to adapt both their skills and themselves for work in a new environment. In practice, one of the most important abilities which the missionary-training programme should develop is an ability which is almost totally denied throughout the normal Western education system, namely the ability to learn from those who have less learning than oneself. This is especially important for practitioners in theology; we need a setting in which those who have experienced formal theological education can learn alongside those who have not — and can learn from them, can share the actual advantages of their lack of expertize. Only if we seriously attempt to do this can we rescue theology from being a field in which the practitioners disable the non-practitioners, and restore it to where Jesus put it, in the hands of ordinary people.[42]

This means that the training institution itself must be thoroughly various and not homogeneous. It is not a seminary. Its community life does not depend on everyone having the same aim, vision, or commitment. Three of the missionary colleges at Selly Oak, including USPG's College of the Ascension, are consciously committed to being plural institutions; they believe that mission training is positively advantaged if it takes place in an institution where there is a substantial proportion of students who are there for quite different purposes, who do not necessarily have any particular missionary or Christian identity. And they believe that there are positive advantages in such training taking place in a context where a large proportion, sometimes a considerable majority, of students are from overseas.

In the college, the missionary disciplines of community have to be worked out. But the possibilities for this are limited. Community necessarily involves some sort of committed sharing in menial work and physical self-maintenance: otherwise, the community life is a luxury enabled by the paid work of those who are not members of the community.

One of the most unfortunate conventions which new missionaries are often expected to accept is the assumption that they are going to be employers of personal domestic servants. In my experience, this issue has caused more controversy among mission students than any other single practical issue. My own view (which I hold very humbly but my wife holds very vigorously) is that it is impossible to be an agent of mission towards domestic servants if one is oneself an employer of domestic servants. In the world as we know it, the conflict of interest between the employing class and the employed class is impossibly great.

But the same problems, in essence, have to be faced within a college which is structured according to the conventions of residential institutions which have grown up in the last century or so in Britain. These conventions are

147

really not much help in preparing people to enter the poorer world: they partake so much of the life-style of the un-poor sections of British culture. I have often thought that, at least for some candidates, a kind of Outward Bound course in self-maintenance and self-reliance would be a good deal more appropriate, or else something more like the simple do-it-yourself community houses which provide accommodation for students at the Urban Theology Unit in Sheffield. Many students are, in any case, highly sensitive to the problem. In fact, there can be few places where the conventions, attitudes, successes and failures of the church are under more rigorous, informed and constructive scrutiny than they are in a missionary training college. Bishop Morgan's comment is potently true:

> The church not only tests but is tested by every call of God to the individual . . . The Candidates Committee and the Training College test and are tested by every missionary candidate committed to their consideration and care. It is extraordinarily easy for committees and colleges to expect of missionary candidates a standard of spiritual life and discipline which it does not occur to them to apply to themselves.[43]

19   The Motive

The Christian movement as a whole is a system of values; the Catholic movement within Anglicanism came into being as an affirmation of these values and as a protest against the danger of losing them.

Any value system, if it is going to be effective, needs to be more than a series of ideas. It needs to be more than a programme of action. It needs affirming and celebrating. It needs devices by which its values take deep root in people's consciousness, at the level where motives work and where changes of attitudes take place. It needs worship and celebration.

Worship is the most obvious aspect of church life in which the Catholic movement has made a difference. For many people, it is the only aspect of church life where it has made a difference, because the doctrinal debates have been conducted in a specialist language which is outside most people's range, and they don't seem to have had much effect on 'real life'. Most of this book has been concerned to show that the doctrine has had and must have an effect on 'real life', and the Oxford Fathers certainly intended that it should. But it remains true that the Catholic movement has had its greatest impact on the conduct of worship; it has made people much more aware of what worship is about. It has made it clear that worship is the main task of the church, rather than social control or moral guardianship or individual compassion.

Catholicism has taught us to see worship as an end in itself, as the supreme human duty. And this is perfectly fair. Worship is our supreme task. But, without wanting to make worship a mere means to an end, or an educational device, one has to ask, worship of what, and why? And the answer must surely be that Christian worship is the affirming of the absolute and ultimate value of God, God as disclosed in Jesus, God who is shown by Jesus to be Father, God who is Spirit, God who is the universal relatedness of the Trinity. And when we start thus to ask what is the nature of the God to whom we accord this supreme value, we find that we cannot acknowledge the value of God without being committed to the purposes which he sets before us. The supreme danger in the Bible is not atheism but idolatry; and idolatry is the constructing and valuing of a deity who fits our needs and suits our preferences.

So worship is a training of our values: no training in mission can be effective without worship. Indeed, it is far truer to say that our training is basically worship, and all that can happen in the classroom is an expanding of the implications of that worship. All the items that can be dealt with in the classroom are limited: all of them depend on some sort of freedom given by external circumstances; none of them is absolutely essential and absolutely universal. The one feature of the church which really can be universal and which can represent its mission in all circumstances, is that the church is a praying presence of the continuing humanity of the Son of God in the world. It is the presence in the world of a group of people who, through persistent and perhaps secret acts of worship, are seeking to bring their values into line with the nature of God, and who therefore are sharing something of God's compassion, anger, and hope for the created order of which they are a part. Everything else is a by-product, situational, contextual, depending on what circumstances allow and enable. But this is the heart of mission, and it is just as possible for the poor, the disabled, the imprisoned, and those whose lives are limited by hostile governments, as it is for the privileged, the able-bodied, and those who can claim the benefits of advanced technology.

Worship is central to mission. So is contemplation, the careful self-emptying of oneself to rest in the awareness of the central truth. But again, one has to ask, contemplation of what, and why? It is possible to have a wonderful feeling of contemplation, but for the whole exercise to be basically self-regarding or, for that matter, self-annihilating. The prayer and contemplation on which Christian mission is based is a meeting with God which does not abolish us but which fulfils us and enables us to take part in the fulfilling of God's purpose. The question which must be put to us in our worship is: Is our worship merely meeting us where we are, placating us and satisfying us in our immaturity and our unwillingness to have our boundaries enlarged? Or it is making demands on our ability to grow, to enter new rooms of meeting, of darkness, of silence, of vision? Even a missionary training college can easily content itself with being a place where people swap views about what they like and are used to. But the college has a duty to educate people to recognize and to value the ways of worship in many parts of the world church; it can give an unrivalled experience of the disturbing and maturing worship which happens when people of many languages and cultures meet as a communiom of saints.

The praying and worshipping presence of Christ in his Body is, more specifically, a eucharistic presence. This is the special Catholic insistence, and it brings both a precision and a flexibility which no other kind of worship can offer. It brings flexibility, because the eucharistic act is less limited by language and culture than other forms of communication which are available to the Christian gospel. I have said that I used to serve a congregation which used at least six different languages: but at the heart of its worship, there was one language which was equally clear and equally mysterious for all, the language of bread broken and wine shared. The Eucharist also brings precision, because it identifies certain quite specific moments and modes of worship to which we have to align our own ideas.

There are two particular eucharistic themes of special significance here, both of which have been dear to the heart of Anglican Catholicism. One is the theme of oblation; the other theme is Eucharist itself.

Oblation has, mercifully, ceased to be a battle-ground

151

between Christians of different emphases. All our modern liturgies make some provision for representing our offering and God's taking of what we are and what we have. What is not offered is not redeemed; but we in Christ offer creation, and ourselves within creation, to be made part of the process of redemption. Therefore, we are valuable, and God affirms our value. We offer ourselves in virtue of Christ's claiming of us. We do not continually insist on our unworthiness: we thank God who makes us worthy to make this offering. So we ourselves are part of the sacrifice.

I have an uneasy feeling that few of those who write learnedly about the eucharistic sacrifice have ever killed their own meat. A missionary in Africa is not likely to be so distant from the real world; he will be involved in feasts even if he doesn't do the killing. And the sacrifice is always a mixture of gladness and sorrow. A life is paid; and (even I know this, who have never killed anything more impressive than a chicken) the thing whose life is offered has to understand why; it has to be told. The community is poorer, too; there is one less animal to be counted in its wealth.

All these feelings go into any real sacrifice. If you offer something, there is a real chance that you won't get it back. But in the total pattern, worked out most precisely in the eucharistic sacrifice, there is a receiving on the far side of the offering, a possessing on the far side of losing.

Quite a lot of people of Catholic inclination have been attracted to Catholicism because Catholicism allows and encourages artistic endeavour and aesthetic sensitivity. All this sort of thing has to be put on the altar by anyone going on overseas mission. You have to be willing to lay aside all sorts of precious cultural standards and interests, and, almost certainly, you may have to lay aside one of the things which English culture tells you is most important, a sense of humour. It may be given back to you later, but in the early days of missionary service there is nothing which more painfully emphasizes the boundaries between cultures than our attempts to be funny. Not only do we laugh at different things: what is far more damaging, the use of humour by those who are powerful or highly literate appears to others as a way of showing who is in charge, or as a way of evading a sensitive issue. Our oblation as missionaries will include all these dangerous treasures. They aren't just thrown away, however, they are offered, into the costly exchange between creator and creature which is summarized in the eucharistic offering.

And we do not offer only our potentially obstructive riches and competences. We offer our ignorance and incompetence. And if there is one thing which can be guaranteed to make clever people feel incompetent, it is their initial inability to speak a new language. But here, in a very practical way, we can see the operation of the principle that we relate to God through others. When I cannot understand the words of the person leading the prayer, my prayer has to move, like the knight in chess, in two directions, sideways *and* upwards. I can't pray direct: I pray by attaching my spiritual energy to that of my brother or sister who is leading the prayer. I trust in the authority and the wisdom of the leader of the prayer, and I pray for that prayer to be heard. I think, in fact, that it's an easier exercise than it sounds: but nothing more truthfully expresses our solidarity in the Gospel together. The offering cannot be made at all unless we make it together.

Our whole self is offered. Nothing can affirm our value more potently than the Eucharist, in which we hear repeatedly that Christ gives his whole self to me, for whom he died. I am loved: I need to be aware of the self who is thus loved, I need to value and recognize my own life with its feelings and instincts and needs: the love of Christ enables me to dare to take the wraps off and to be myself on a wider and freer scale. And yet this self-awareness has to be offered too. Self-awareness can be an unhallowed pre-occupation, a licensed egocentricity. The charity of Christ requires also a certain self-*un*awareness, a willingness not to have, a trust that secure having comes not by holding but on the far side of losing. A more ordinary word for self-unawareness is courage, which has its own place in missionary motive, and has a way of showing up in improbable people and places. Those of us who talk best and have the most attractive ideas quite often have good reason to be somewhere else on the day when action really happens.

The other great theme of Eucharist is Eucharist itself. In spite of our long chapter on confrontation, the missionary is never primarily an accuser: the missionary is a thanker, a 'eucharister'. She sees and selects and celebrates what is good, what is in accord with the purpose of the Creator. She does not lightly overlook the disorder, the injustice and the pain. But her motive is basically eucharistic: she is able to affirm and recognize that which calls out thankfulness, and therefore she will not only draw the attention of others to these things, she will attack all that conceals and denies the thankworthiness of creation.

The missionary community, very simply, is a community that is placed in the world to give thanks, and which will not rest until everyone else can honestly and justifiably give thanks also. And here again, the catholicity of our mission is its guideline. What you feel thankful for tells us who you are. You give thanks for your health, or your sanity — but in doing so you are distinguishing yourself from those who do not have health or sanity to be thankful for. You give thanks for your success in exams or in getting a job — when you know that the system depends on some being failures. You give thanks for your Christian faith and membership, and this also can be a thankfulness that we are not as others are. It is not wrong to give thanks for what we count as blessings, but this is not the eucharistic thanksgiving. The great thanksgiving in the Eucharist requires us not to be thankful for the things which distinguish us from others, but for those things that we have in common with others, our createdness at the hand of God, and the action of God in Christ and through the Holy Spirit towards us and towards the whole human race. The Eucharist is a disciplining and a training of our motive and our self-image, so that we find ourselves able to say, and to mean deeply, the simple prayer of Thomas Merton, 'Thank God that I *am* as other men are'.[44]

The eucharistic thanksgiving depends entirely on the

nature of God disclosed by Jesus. It is an approach to the Father through the Son. When Jesus says that no one can come to the Father except through him, he is not knocking everyone else on the head and saying that no one else can possibly know anything about God (John 14:6). He is saying that only a Son can say of his Father, This is Father. All the miracles, even the resurrection, could be pieces of technological wizardry with no real hope for anyone: what is important about them is that they are done by the one who brings us to God as a son brings his friends to his father, and in the process they are made not just friends but adopted brothers and sisters (Galatians 4:5).

All mission is the spreading outwards of that relationship between Father and Son which is quite specifically Christian and is the whole basis of the Eucharist, both in our offering and in God's self-giving. But the thanksgiving is for what has been done for all, not just for those who at present know the benefit of it. The Mass is not offered just for the congregation, it is offered for the parish. Those who know they are chosen are chosen for those who do not know they are chosen. The church is for the whole nation, it is not just an instrument in the hands of those who happen to have the power to form the state. The Body of Christ is in the world not for its own growth or its own satisfaction, but to be the means by which people are saved through community and into community.

The Catholic witness, particularly within Anglicanism, requires the church to be clear about its purpose and identity as church, precisely in order that it may be better able to represent the reckless and unbounded generosity of God's grace. 'God pours out his grace through very leaky buckets.' The bucket must not seek praise for its beauty or efficiency. It has got to be a bucket; it has got to have a structure, so that it can be taken to where it is needed. But it must not hold its contents to itself as a private treasure. By God's mercy, it will leak, and one day be so full of holes that, as a distinct thing, it will cease to exist. And the Eucharist prepares us to expect and to treasure that kind of holiness. Perhaps this is the most difficult discipline for any person or group that is active in mission; yet it is at the heart of Christ's self-giving, when he says not only, 'This is my body, broken,' but also, 'Take, eat'; share in this brokenness, this sacrifice, yourselves. Of all our new liturgies, the one which most powerfully claims the eucharistic symbols is that of the Episcopal Church in Scotland: at this moment of the Breaking of the Bread, the point where the cost and the hope of the missionary enterprise are made most clear, the word of the priest expounds the missionary commitment of every Eucharist:

> 'We break this bread,
> Seal of communion in Christ's Body once broken,
> Pledge that his church may be the wheat which bears
> its fruit in dying.'

And the people of God respond:

> 'Lord unite us in this sign.'

Notes

1 Reprinted by permission of Faber and Faber Ltd from *The Anathemata* by David Jones.

2 John V. Taylor, *The Primal Vision* (SCM Press, London, 1963); *The Go-Between God* (SCM Press, London, 1972).

3 Lesslie Newbigin, *The Open Secret* (SPCK, London, 1978).

4 Owen Chadwick (ed.), *The Mind of the Oxford Movement* (A. & C. Black, London, 1960), p. 147.

5 *To a Rebellious House?* Report of the Church of England's Partners in Mission Consultation (Church Information Office, London, 1981), p. 22.

6 A. M. Allchin, *The Dynamic of Tradition* (Darton, Longman & Todd, London, 1981), p. 28.

7 Basil Moore (ed.), *Black Theology* (C. Hurst, London, 1973).

8 J. V. Taylor, *The Primal Vision*, pp. 15ff.

9 Ignatius of Antioch, *Letter to the Ephesians*, 19, quoted in J. C. Fenton, *The Gospel of St Matthew* (Penguin Books, Harmondsworth, 1963), p. 46. See also W. K. Lowther Clarke, *Divine Humanity* (SPCK, London, 1936), pp. 41ff.

10 Ambrose Reeves, *Justice in South Africa* (Africa Bureau, London, 1955), p. 5.

11 H. Maynard Smith, *Frank, Bishop of Zanzibar* (SPCK, London, 1926), pp. 242ff.

12 Ibid., p. 302

13 W. G. Peck, *The Social Implications of the Oxford Movement* (Charles Scribner's Sons, New York and London, 1933), p. 67.

14 Essay by W. V. Lucas, 'The Christian Approach to Non-Christian Customs', in E. R. Morgan (ed.), *Essays Catholic and Missionary* (SPCK, London, 1928), pp. 115ff.

15 W. G. Peck, *The Social Implications of the Oxford Movement*, p. 66.

16 Ibid., p. 68.

17 Hugh Latimer, *Sermons* (Parker Society/Cambridge University Press, 1844), pp. 249ff.

18 E. R. Morgan, *The Catholic Revival and Missions*, (SPG, London, 1933), pp. 15ff.

19 Ibid., p. 19.

20 Anthony Barker, *Giving and Receiving* (Faith Press, London, 1959).

21 *North-South: A Programme for Survival* (Pan Books, London, 1980).

22 L. Wickremesinghe, *Mission, Politics and Evangelism* (Church Missionary Society, London, 1979), p. 9.

23 Peck, *The Social Implications of the Oxford Movement*, p. 94.

24 *Spirit of God, Spirit of Christ*: Ecumenical Reflections on the *Filioque* Controversy (SPCK/World Council of Churches, Geneva, 1981); see also Vladimir Lossky, *In the Image and Likeness of God*, (A. R. Mowbray, Oxford, 1975), pp. 71ff and Basil Moore, *Black Theology*, pp. 8ff and 119ff.

25 For a much more thorough development of the main theme of the following section, see Lesslie Newbigin, *The Open Secret*, pp. 73–101.

26 Leslie Stradling, *The Acts through Modern Eyes* (A. R. Mowbray, Oxford, 1963), p. 13.

27 Ibid., p. 3.

28 Martin Jarrett-Kerr, CR, *Patterns of Christian Acceptance* (Oxford University Press, London, 1972), p. 291.

29 Essay by Philip Loyd, 'The Church at Home', in Morgan (ed.), *Essays Catholic and Missionary*, p. 317.

30 Essay by Edward Patterson, 'Giving and Receiving in Art', in E. R. Morgan and Roger Lloyd (eds.), *The Mission of the Anglican Communion* (SPCK & SPG, London, 1948), pp. 196ff.

31 Adrian Hastings, *African Christianity* (Geoffrey Chapman, London and Dublin, 1976), p. 48.

32 Julius K. Nyerere, 'Education for Self-Reliance', in *The Ecumenical Review*, vol. XIX, no. 4 (World Council of Churches, Geneva, October 1967), p. 392.

33 Maynard Smith, *Frank, Bishop of Zanzibar*, p. 258.

34 John Davies, *Good News in Galatians* (Collins — Fontana, London, 1975), pp. 26–8 and 58.

35 E. W. Southcott, *The Parish Comes Alive* (A. R. Mowbray, London, 1956), pp. 58ff and 148.

36 Essay by M. Gibbard, SSJE, 'Catholics in the World Church', in John Wilkinson (ed.), *Catholic Anglicans Today* (Darton Longman & Todd, London, 1968), p. 205.

37 Maynard Smith, *Frank, Bishop of Zanzibar*, pp. 129ff; Jarrett-Kerr, *Patterns of Christian Acceptance*, pp. 232ff.

38 *To a Rebellious House?*, p. 28.

39 A. M. Allchin, *The World is a Wedding* (Darton, Longman & Todd, London, 1978), p. 161.

40 Ned Thomas, *The Welsh Extremist* (Victor Gollancz, London, 1971), p. 125.

41 C. G. Jung, *The Integration of the Personality*, trans. Stanley Dell (Kegan Paul, Trench, Trubner, London, 1940), p. 295.

42 Ian M. Fraser, *Reinventing Theology as the People's Work* (I. M. Fraser & USPG, London, 1981), pp. 4ff.

43 Essay by E. R. Morgan, 'Missionary Vocation and Training', in Morgan (ed.), *Essays Catholic and Missionary*, p. 244.

44 Allchin, *The World is a Wedding*, p. 100.

Stories, illustrations, etc., not otherwise acknowledged are from colleagues, students, and other friends in USPG, Selly Oak, South Africa, and St Asaph Diocese, and from my own experience.

Index